THE GIFT OF MIRACLES

The Gift of Miracles

*Experiencing God's Extraordinary
Power in Your Life*

Robert DeGrandis, S.S.J.
with
Linda Schubert

Servant Publications
Ann Arbor, Michigan

Other Books by Robert DeGrandis, S.S.J.

Praying for Miracles
Come, Follow Me
Resting in the Spirit
Renewed by the Holy Spirit
Coming to Life
Healing the Broken Heart
Word of Knowledge
Intergenerational Healing
Healing through the Mass
Growing in Jesus
The Gift of Tongues
The Gift of Prophecy
Inner Healing through Stations of the Cross
Introduction to the Catholic Charismatic Renewal
To Forgive is Divine
*Forgiveness and Inner Healing**
*Healing of Self-Image**

* with Betty Tapscott

Excerpts from Scripture are taken from the New International Version
version of the Bible, copyright © 1978 by New York International Bible
Society, used by permission of Zondervan Bible Publishers

Unless otherwise noted, most quoted material in this book is from
an unpublished study conducted by the author in 1990.

Published by Servant Publications
P.O. Box 8617
Ann Arbor, Michigan 48107

Cover design by Charles Piccirilli and Bob Coe

    93 94 95 10 9 8 7 6 5 4 3

Printed in the United States of America
ISBN 0-89283-728-4

Library of Congress Cataloging-in-Publication Data

DeGrandis, Robert.
    The gift of miracles : experiencing God's extraordinary
power in your life / Robert DeGrandis, with Linda Schubert.
        p.   cm.
    Includes bibliographical references.
    ISBN 0-89283-728-4
    1. Miracles. I. Schubert, Linda. II. Title.
BT97.2.D44   1991
231.7'3—dc20   91-23970
                                                    CIP

I pray… that the eyes of your heart may be enlightened in order that you may know the hope to which he has called you, the riches of his glorious inheritance in the saints, and his incomparably great power for us who believe….

Ephesians 1:18-19

Contents

PART I

OUR MIRACLE HERITAGE

If you belong to Christ, then you are Abraham's seed, and heirs according to the promise.

Galatians 3:29

ONE

Longing for Miracles

O divine Spirit… renew in our own days Your miracles as of a Second Pentecost…   **Pope John XXIII, 1959**[1]

The Appeal of Miracles. Miracles have a universal attraction. From every walk of life, every age, every circumstance, we find people drawn to them. Since childhood I, myself, have been fascinated with them. People often tell me of their yearning to believe in miracles. They seem to touch something very deep in the core of our being.

Consider the story of 70-year-old Hilario Valdes who was healed of blindness. He said, "… I came today to give thanks to Jesus for his great mercy on me. I have not been grateful in my life, but now I want to give thanks with all my heart, and to praise God before everyone because he has healed me and given me new eyes."[2]

Or ponder the story of Karen, as told by her mother, L.H. in Washington State: "My daughter Karen was born mentally and emotionally handicapped due to brain damage in the womb which occurred at the death of her twin. At age 30 she could read isolated words at about a third-grade level. One night during a prayer meeting she suddenly cried out, 'Hey, guys, God healed my brain!' Someone handed her a Bible and asked her to read and explain a passage, something she had not been able to do previously. She read the verse, understood it, and explained it clearly. She told the group that during praise and worship she received a picture in her mind of a big needle and thread, and knew that God was 'sewing up her brain.'

"Sometime later she took three college courses and received all Bs. Today, as she serves the Lord, her insights into people are simple, clear, and beautiful."

Our Emphasis. Scripture is filled with miracle stories, in both the Old and New Testaments. It is in the New Testament, however, that we find miracles listed as a gift, or charism, of the Holy Spirit. The gift of miracles, and the other charisms listed with it, are ways in which ordinary Christians reveal, or manifest, the presence of Jesus in the world.

> Now to each one the manifestation of the Spirit is given for the common good. To one there is given through the Spirit the message of wisdom, to another the message of knowledge by means of the same Spirit, to another faith by the same Spirit, to another gifts of healing by that one Spirit, to another miraculous powers, to another prophecy, to another distinguishing between spirits, to another speaking in different kinds of tongues, and to still another the interpretation of tongues. **1 Corinthians 12:7-10**

The stories of Hilario and Karen may reflect one of the kinds of miracles Pope John XXIII asked for when he prayed, "… renew in our own days Your miracles as of a Second Pentecost…." They are examples of some of the things we will talk about in this book, where the charismatic gift of miracles flows through ordinary people in a healing environment. As we can see from the prayer by John XXIII, prayers for healing and miracles are integral to our Catholic theology and tradition. Our focus is upon the gift of miracles in the lives of ordinary people in this day and age. This is not intended to be a theological textbook on miracles, but rather an easy-reading introductory study.

Goal for This Book. What I expect the Lord to do through this book is to create in the reader two things: a deeper desire to yield to the miracle ministry of the Holy Spirit; and a greater expectation for miracles.

When we yield to the Lord who is love, we find he wants to bless us more than we want to be blessed. 1 John 4:16 defines God as love. The notion of love generally connotes healing. Everyone wants wholeness for children and spouse, and God wants the same. When we open our hearts we will find he will frequently move through us in dramatic ways, as some of the examples in this book attest.

When we know how much he loves us, and surrender to that love, it becomes easier to expect miracles. The word "expect" is intimately connected to our knowledge that God is love. Expectancy opens the door of faith. When the door of faith is wide open, possibilities are unlimited.

The Lord tells us that we, his friends and coworkers, are to go out and proclaim the good news; and that he will equip us for this service. "May the God of peace, who through the blood of the eternal covenant brought back from the dead our Lord Jesus... equip you with everything good for doing his will..." (Hebrews 13:20-21). He promises that signs and wonders will follow. "And these signs will accompany those who believe: In my name they will drive out demons; they will speak in new tongues; they will pick up snakes with their hands; and when they drink deadly poison, it will not hurt them at all; they will place their hands on sick people, and they will get well" (Mark 16:17-18). Let us surrender to the God of love, yield to the ministry of the Holy Spirit, and expect great things!

Without the Gifts. In my travels I hear many discouraging reports of declining attendance at Mass, priests leaving active ministry, and young people staying away from church. Many have left for other Christian churches, drawn by the emphasis on Scripture, powerful preaching, and manifestations of healings and miracles. Others have been drawn into various cults and occult groups.

Our church has been weakened by its failure to nurture the charismatic gifts, given to us by the Holy Spirit to strengthen and build up the Body of Christ. The *Constitution on the Church* states: "It is not only through the sacraments and church ministries that the same Holy Spirit sanctifies and leads the People of God and enriches it with virtues. Allotting His gifts 'to everyone according as he wills' (1 Corinthians 12:11). He distributes special graces among the faithful of every rank. By these gifts He makes them fit and ready to undertake the various tasks or offices advantageous for the renewal and upbuilding of the Church...."[3]

To the extent that this strengthening dimension is lacking in the church, Catholics can become susceptible to questionable spiritual experiences from sources hostile to the Christian gospel. New Age is a good example. I heard a story one time about a young Catholic girl from the Boston, Massachusetts area, who moved to Miami, Florida, to start a school for witches. She said that as a Catholic she felt her prayers weren't being answered. When she got involved in the occult she received many more answers to prayer. A time will come, the Lord reminds us, when men and women "will turn their ears away from the truth and turn aside to myths" (2 Timothy 4:4). This seems particularly applicable to our day and age. God has given us powerful charismatic gifts to bring healing to the Body of Christ. As we stay centered on him and allow him to keep our motives pure, we will not be seduced by promises of power from non-Christian sources.

The Challenge. These facts challenge us to get on our knees and pray for a new Pentecost in the Catholic church. We are confronted with the need for restoration of the power given to us in our spiritual heritage. There must come a time when these gifts are active within the church and within every parish community. We need to see the gifts of healing and miracles (like the experience of Mercedes and Karen) in every community. People are drawn to healing services for relief from pain and suffering in spirit, mind, and body. They come crying and begging for help for their families and loved ones. The merciful miracle ministry of Jesus Christ needs to be evident everywhere there is a Christian and a need. Our hurting people need to know that he is truly here to give life. "... I have come that they may have life, and have it to the full" (John 10:10).

The gospel has become so watered down that some Christians don't believe the Lord can, or even wants to, help them. Some years ago in Kingston, Jamaica, I shared my beliefs about healing with a group of Catholic and Protestant seminarians. They agreed in principle that God heals, but when we prayed over a Protestant seminarian with a terrible toothache, and he was healed, most of them shook their heads in unbelief. Many can accept theory but have trouble with practice. An important purpose of miracles is that people come to know the power of Christ once more, to believe in him, and to surrender to his loving ministry on their behalf. People need to know that when Jesus walked the earth everyone who came to him for healing was healed. He's the same today; he hasn't changed. It is my deeply held belief that everyone who has ever or will ever come to Jesus for healing has already or will be healed in some way—on Jesus' terms and in his time.

A Basic Assumption. Some people say, "Maybe it isn't God's will for me to be happy, healthy, and whole. Maybe

I'm supposed to suffer." A basic assumption of mine is that God wants people to be happy, healthy, and whole. Yet not all people are happy, healthy, and whole. Scripture reminds us that God *wants* all people saved in the kingdom of heaven; yet probably not all people will be saved because God respects our free will, and many certainly seem to choose not to follow God and his ways. "... God our Savior... wants all men to be saved and to come to a knowledge of the truth" (1 Timothy 2:3-4). Full salvation, according to true liberation theology, is that Jesus came to save us from all evil: spiritual, psychological, physical, social, economic (see Acts 10:38). Therefore, we continually try to appropriate what Jesus gained for us on the cross through praying for healing of mind, spirit, body, social situations, financial conditions, etc. We are called to continually reach out for his perfect will, and to cooperate with him in bringing that will to pass.

To Help You Believe. Most of the testimonies included in this book came in response to a "Miracle Survey" conducted in various parts of the country (see Chapter 9). The respondents shared some very personal and powerful stories, many of which can be found in a companion volume, *Praying for Miracles: A workbook approach.*[4] Most of the stories have never been scientifically proven; few would qualify for a "Lourdes-type" official documentation. They are, however, deeply moving personal stories shared by everyday people who have met God at the point of their need.

The testimonies can help greatly in opening your spirit to what is possible in God. That is because personal testimonies get you emotionally involved, while enabling you to draw your own conclusions. Although some people have a fear of being opened emotionally to testimonies of fellow Christians, most have no fear of becoming emotionally involved in television programs such as soap operas, football games, even news events, and mini-series. The human person is body, mind, and spirit, and needs to be opened in every way for God's love and healing. We live to a great degree by our emotions. Witness the Catholics who support the pro-choice movement, even though the church states that abortion is morally wrong. This is a highly emotional issue.

When people fall in love it is primarily an emotional drawing, which often leads to a lifelong commitment. St. Alphonsus Liguori (1696-1787) said that no sinner would ever be converted unless he had a deep experience of God's love. Emotional involvement with people opens our spirits to them. Emotional involvement in spiritual testimonies can open our spirits more to Jesus.

Take time with these stories. Ponder them. Allow the Holy Spirit to teach you through the experiences of your brothers and sisters in Christ. They share their stories to help you believe. "... he testifies so that you also may believe" (John 19:35).

In Response to Requests. Many people have told me they want some direction on how to cooperate with God in manifesting the gift of miracles. Many asked for practical suggestions about handling their own skepticism. All wanted lots of personal stories. In response to these requests, this book is divided into three parts: (1) "Our Miracle Heritage," which includes some theological foundations; (2) "Entering In," which covers areas of yielding and responding to the Spirit; a question and answer section; survey responses; and a comprehensive prayer to release negativity and open the door to the gift of miracles; (3) "To God Be the Glory," which includes testimonies and a concluding prayer. In the Appendix we have included a list of the miracles of Jesus. Meditation on these Scripture accounts can open your heart to this key dimension of Jesus' ministry, and help you believe that what he has done for others, he also wants to do for you.

A priest who responded to the survey added this note to the bottom of his questionnaire: "Father DeGrandis, I want you to write and publish this book on miracles far and wide, so more of God's suffering children will turn with full confidence to the Lord for release from their sufferings and sorrow."

A Catholic's Personal Miracle History. Most Catholics, I believe, have experienced miracles. Perhaps it was simply the instant healing of a headache, or a bad situation remedied in an amazing way. Most people have probably experienced miracles, because the Holy Spirit is much more actively involved in people's lives than they realize. We can become so caught up in things of the world that his loving, energizing presence goes unnoticed.

Many times when I have asked Catholics about miracles in their lives, they get a faraway look in their eyes and recall simple, moving stories of the Lord's loving involvement in difficult situations. Those memories linger for a lifetime. Often when the Lord intervenes to meet a physical need, he meets a deep need of the heart at the same time. Even a lesser miracle can have a life-changing effect.

In the broader sense, though, many have touched the miraculous. Our entry into Christianity is miraculous; every sacrament contains the miraculous; baptism in the Holy Spirit is miraculous. Every charismatic gift is miraculous. Every encounter with Jesus is miraculous. However, these types of moral miracles are not visible.

As we focus our attention specifically on the charismatic gift of miracles, let's be aware of our personal miracle history with Jesus. Allow those experiences to be catalysts and stepping stones to build greater faith. God cared enough to help you then, whenever it was; he still cares enough to help you now.

Little Before the Lord. Let's ask the Lord to draw us close to him as little children. "Anyone who will not receive the kingdom of God like a little child will never enter it" (Mark 10:15). As we become very little before the Lord we create an openness that allows a free flow of his Spirit. It's a matter of innocence, and an awareness of our personal inability apart from God. It is an attitude of heart of absolute confidence, a position of adoration while allowing him total sovereignty. With this posture, we have less standing in the way of the Lord's gift. We are wide-open channels.

KEY POINTS

- Miracles have a universal appeal.
- Jesus promises signs and equips his coworkers for miracles.
- The church is weakened and more vulnerable when charismatic, manifestation gifts are lacking.
- Manifestation gifts are given to strengthen the church.
- Without charismatic gifts we are more vulnerable to spiritual experiences hostile to the gospel.
- Our challenge is to bring more satisfying religious experience to the church.
- We need to know that the power of Jesus Christ is available today.
- Prayers for healing and miracles are integral to our Catholic theology and tradition.
- We all play a part in bringing Jesus' power to others.
- Most Christians can recall miracles in their lives.
- We are invited to approach the Lord as little children.

PRAYER

Come, Spirit of wisdom, and give us divine assistance to slip off our worldly coats, any adult skepticism, any family patterns of unbelief, and sit humbly in your presence. We want to learn from you.

Lord, there is a deep longing in your church for spiritual power. Release that power, Lord. Breathe on us, Holy Spirit, with the breath of Pentecost. Thank you, Lord. Amen.

TWO

What Is a Miracle?

These charismatic gifts, whether they be the most outstand-
ing or the more simple and widely diffused, are to be re-
ceived with thanksgiving and consolation, for they are
exceedingly suitable and useful for the needs of the Church.
Dogmatic Constitution on the Church[1]

I Had My Doubts. In a large healing service one time I received a word of knowledge that someone's ovaries were being healed. When I spoke out the word, a man in the back
raised his hand and said, "That's me!" After the crowd qui-
eted down and the laughter stopped, I said to the group,
"Now that would really have been a miracle!"

If We Were to Ask. If we were to go back into the Old
Testament to the time of Abraham and ask Sarah the question, "What is a miracle?" she would probably point to her
son Isaac, born when she was in her nineties (Genesis 17:17,
21:7).
    If we were to question the thirsty Israelites in the Desert of
Zin, they would point to the waters of Meribah (Numbers
20:13) and say, "Now, that's a miracle!" If we were to question the priests carrying the ark of the covenant, they would
point to the dry path through the overflowing Jordan river
(Joshua 3:15-16) and say, "Now, that's a miracle!" If we were

to ask the widow at Zarephath, she would point to her son, restored to life by Elijah's prayers (1 Kings 17:22). If we were to ask the people of Jericho, they would point to the fallen wall (Joshua 6:20); Daniel would point to the closed mouths of the lions (Daniel 6:22); the three young men in the fiery furnace would point to the fourth man (Daniel 3:25).

If we were to ask young Mary in Nazareth the question, "What is a miracle?" she would point to the child in her womb (Luke 1:35). If we were to ask the royal official's son (John 4:46), the demoniac (Mark 1:26), and Peter's mother-in-law (Matthew 8:14), they would point to the wonders performed by Jesus in their lives.

After the crucifixion, if we were to ask Peter, James, John, Mary Magdalene, and the mother of Jesus the question, "What is a miracle?" they would point to the empty tomb (Luke 24:2).

The Empty Tomb. When I was studying the question, "What is a miracle?" what struck me immediately was the simple truth that our church is founded on a miracle: the resurrection of Jesus Christ. To be a Christian, to be a Catholic, is to believe in miracles; they are central to our salvation history. When we say the creed at Sunday Mass we are saying we believe in miracles; we believe in the power flowing from Christ's resurrection; we believe in the creator of heaven and earth; we believe Jesus was conceived by the power of the Holy Spirit; we believe he descended to the dead and rose to heaven and is seated with the Father. We believe in miracles. "Praise be to the God and Father of our Lord Jesus Christ! In his great mercy he has given us new birth into a living hope through the resurrection of Jesus Christ from the dead" (1 Peter 1:3).

Official Teaching of the Church. Some of the teaching of the Catholic church concerning miracles was outlined at the First Vatican Council (1869-70). After defining faith, the

Council stated: "Nevertheless, so that the obeisance of our faith (our worship) might be consonant with reason, God has been pleased to supply, besides the interior aids of the Holy Spirit, external evidences of his revelation, namely divine acts, especially miracles and prophecies. In splendidly displaying God's omnipotence and infinite knowledge, these constitute most certain signs of divine revelation, attuned to the understanding of all men."[2] The Council further stated: "If anyone should say that all miracles are impossible and that consequently all accounts of them, even though found in the Holy Scriptures, are to be taken as fabulous and mythical, or that miracles can never be known with certainty, and that they do not provide valid proofs of the divine origin of the Christian religion: let him be anathema."[3]

The Vatican II documents state: "When Jesus rose up again after suffering death on the cross for mankind, He manifested that He had been appointed Lord, Messiah, and Priest forever (cf. Acts 2:36, Hebrews 5:6; 7:17-21), and He poured out on His disciples the Spirit promised by the Father (cf. Acts 2:33). The Church, consequently, equipped with the gifts of her Founder and faithfully guarding His precepts of charity, humility, and self-sacrifice, receives the mission to proclaim and to establish among all peoples the kingdom of Christ and of God."[4]

An Interpretation of the Official Teaching. Louis Monden, S.J., in *Signs and Wonders,* further interprets the teaching of the church: "It requires that we believe in the possibility of the miraculous and in its probative value; but it leaves each mind free to judge the worth of any particular miracle, as such."[5]

If we believe in a personal God, we believe in miracles. We believe in a personal God who is love, and love always seeks what is best for the beloved. Our Father invites us to prayer and faith to move mountains. Jesus was a perfect reflection of the Father and he worked many recorded miracles (see list of Jesus' Miracles in the appendix). "... these signs will accompany those who believe: In my name they will drive out demons; they will speak in new tongues; they will pick up snakes with their hands; and when they drink deadly poison, it will not hurt them at all; they will place their hands on sick people, and they will get well" (Mark 16:17-18). Faith not only moves mountains; it also moves kidney stones.

Miracles Necessary for Saints to be Canonized. Throughout church history, miraculous healings have been especially associated with the saints. The book *Nothing Short of a Miracle* lists seven criteria, set down by Pope Benedict XIV, for an authentic church-named miracle that makes a saint eligible for beatification and later canonization. The seven criteria are:

1. The disease must be serious and impossible (or at least very difficult) to cure by human means.
2. The disease must not be in a stage at which it is liable to disappear shortly by itself.
3. Either no medical treatment must have been given or it must be certain that the treatment given has no reference to the cure.
4. The cure must be instantaneous.
5. The cure must be complete.
6. The cure must be permanent.
7. The cure must not be preceded by a crisis of a sort which would make it possible that the cure was wholly or partially natural.[6]

A Few of the Saints. Included below are several references to miracles in the lives of the saints:

St. Clare of Montefalco (1268-1308): "Her life... was distinguished by the performance of miracles, the spirit of prophecy, and a singular understanding of divine mysteries...."

St. Didacus of Alcala (1400-1463): "... he was assigned to

the monastery in Alcala (Spain) where he was revered for his many miracles."

Blessed Anthony Bonfadini (1402-1482): "At the age of thirty-nine, he abandoned his comfortable existence to join the Franciscan Order and, having obtained his doctorate in theology, was ordained a priest. He became a renowned preacher throughout Italy and a zealous missionary in the Holy Land, his labors being crowned with innumerable conversions and miracles."

St. Francis Xavier (1506-1552): One of the original followers of St. Ignatius Loyola, he "performed many miracles, was granted the gift of tongues... healed countless persons, established churches in remote areas, and is reported to have raised several persons from the dead."

Saint Pacifico of San Severino (1653-1721): "The saint was endowed with many supernatural gifts. He was often found in ecstasy while celebrating Holy Mass, and his countenance at those times would shine like the sun. He had the gift of prophecy and often healed the sick."

St. Teresa Margaret of the Sacred Heart (1747-1770): "During the time she served as infirmarian, many of the sick were miraculously cured when she blessed them with oil from the lamps that burned before the statues of Our Lady and St. Joseph."[7]

St. John Marie Vianney (1786-1859) better known as the Cure d'Ars: "...after the death of this great nineteenth-century miracle worker, from many claimed cures only thirty were sent to Rome. But each of these was of a caliber to potentially qualify as an official beatification miracle."[8]

St. Charbel Makhlouf (1828-1898): Numerous, well-authenticated miracles have been performed at the shrine (where his body rests, free of corruption). After the exhumation of 1950, the monastery began keeping records of the miracles and within a two-year period had collected over one thousand two hundred reports. The most publicized miracle is one involving a fifty-year-old seamstress, Miss

Mountaha Daher of Bekassin, Lebanon, who had been a hunchback since childhood. After a visit to the shrine during which she prayed, not for herself but for needy relatives, she had the figure of a woman with normal proportions.[9]

Definitions to Consider. *Webster's Seventh New Collegiate Dictionary* defines a miracle as "an extraordinary event manifesting a supernatural work of God; an extremely outstanding or unusual event, thing or accomplishment."[10]

The Maryknoll Catholic Dictionary, First American Edition, defines a miracle as "an observable effect in the moral or physical order which is in contravention to natural laws and which cannot be explained by any natural power but only by the power of God."[11]

After reviewing the many formal definitions, I would suggest that we call miracles dramatic answers to prayer. They seem to be normally instantaneous manifestations of the Spirit, doing that which is outside of God's ordinary ways of doing things but which has an appropriate place in his plan.

The charismatic gift of healing, on the other hand, includes a much broader definition. Healings are also answers to prayer, but generally less dramatic in manifestation and not as distinguishable from natural means.

Counterfeit Miracles. These generally occur in an environment in which people are not surrendered to Jesus Christ, but are seeking power apart from him. Supernatural power displayed through an individual outside of a personal relationship with the Lord Jesus Christ could fall into the realm of magic. Magic is a general term used in reference to counterfeit miracles produced through witchcraft, evil spirits, or various occult practices. "The coming of the lawless one will be in accordance with the work of Satan displayed in all kinds of counterfeit miracles, signs and wonders, and in every sort of evil that deceives those who are perishing...." (2 Thessalonians 2:9-10).

The grace of God touched one woman after she read of healings occurring through people's faith in various New Age practices and powers not submitted to Jesus Christ. She mused, "How can they who have so little believe so much?" Turning to God she asked, "How can I who have so much believe so little?" As she asked the question God poured into her spirit a fresh gift of faith.

New Testament Words for Miracle. The Latin word *miraculum* comes from *mirari,* meaning "to wonder." It means "a wonderful event."[12] The Greek word *dunamis* (meaning power, inherent ability) is used in Scripture to describe "works of a supernatural origin and character, such as could not be produced by natural agents and means."[13] The Greek word *semeion* (a sign, a mark) refers to miracles and wonders as signs of divine authority. Might, power, work, sign, and wonder are words frequently used in connection with miracles. "God also testified to it by signs, wonders, and various miracles, and gifts of the Holy Spirit distributed according to his will" (Hebrews 2:4).

Charism of the Holy Spirit. Monsignor Vincent Walsh in *Lead my People* speaks of charismatic gifts as "actions of God whereby he uses a person as an instrument of grace for another." He continues, "Every true charism begins with God, who is close to us and extremely active in drawing all people to himself. Therefore, to say that charisms are 'actions of God' doesn't mean they are not daily and regular occurrences. It does mean that we 'awaken' to God, wait on God, and put aside our human way of acting and thinking… the charisms are not 'voices from heaven' or direct divine intervention (although these can occur). They are powers God gives to one person to help others. They are regular, normal parts of God's plan whereby the Body of Christ is equipped to help its members."[14]

Miracles are listed as one of nine manifestation gifts of

charisms of the Holy Spirit (1 Corinthians 12:7-10). These gifts are categorized by some authors, both Catholic and Protestant, as follows:

Intellectual gifts: wisdom, knowledge, and discernment
Word gifts: tongues, interpretation of tongues, and
   prophecy
Power gifts: faith, healing, and miracles

Resident Within. In my travels around the world in leadership training and healing services, I have given many workshops on gifts of the Holy Spirit, including the gift of miracles. What has proven true is that the gifts (promised in Scripture) are given in the sacrament of confirmation and released through baptism in the Holy Spirit. As the Holy Spirit comes in power, his gifts begin to flow. In the workshops as people listen, receive, and respond, the charismatic gifts become operative. As the participants continue to yield, they find the gifts blossoming in their lives and ministries. Some people may develop ministries in specific gifts (using them predominantly), but each gift is generally available as needs arise.

An Illustration. To illustrate how the Lord shows his power through us I will use the image of a light bulb. Within the light bulb itself is a filament, which is made of material intentionally designed to react to electricity in a certain way. When the light is switched on, electricity surges through the filament, which begins to glow, until it is hidden by the bright light shining from it. The filament fulfills its purpose by providing a path for the electricity. When the power is switched off, the filament is still there, ready to be used again.

As we allow the Holy Spirit to flow through us, he uses our identity in much the same way that electricity uses the filament. God designed each of us to be used by him in a certain way. Then, because we are more than objects to him, he honors us by asking our permission to use us, by inviting us to work *with* him. He is the light; we shine with his brightness. In the process, we become more ourselves than we ever could without him. This is the ultimate goal for our Christian lives. "…I am in my Father, and you are in me, and I am in you" (John 14:20).

What is a Miracle? If Helen C. of California were asked, "What is a miracle?" she would point to a woman's unborn child: "A friend called and told me that an ultrasound test showed that her unborn grandchild had a gap between the esophagus and the stomach. They were not properly joined. I prayed, and asked the Lord to give me a picture of that area in perfect health. Knowing that he was there when the child was formed in the womb, I prayed that the light of Christ would act as a beam of light carrying the life directly from God to this child as a lifeline, sealing the gap between the stomach and esophagus. I also prayed for a healing in the child's relationship with his mother, and for forgiveness to flow between mother and child. One week later the follow-up test revealed the esophagus properly joined to the stomach. No one could say why it happened."

If Mary Forest of Oceanside, California, were asked, "What is a miracle?" she would think back to a certain day on Ellis Island: "My family was detained on Ellis Island when we arrived as immigrants because of ulcers on my eyes. I was only three years old, and had bandages on my eyes. After mom washed my eyes with holy water, they were healed."

If you were to ask Evelyn Byrd Fagan of Santa Rosa, California, "What is a miracle?" she would tell this story: "When I was driving down the precarious mountain road from my home in an isolated region of the northern California coast, I suddenly met another car coming up. When I jammed on my brakes, they locked, causing me to go spinning off the cliff in a semicircle. As my car went hurtling straight down a 45-degree slope I asked, 'Lord, where are we going?' The car immediately came to a stop, long enough for me to get my purse and climb out. Once I was out, the car continued down the hill until it hit a tree. I was unhurt, and when the tow truck driver pulled the car up the cliff we discovered that it too was unhurt."

If Doris A. from Leucadia, California, were asked, "What is a miracle?" she would point to the miraculous restoration of her dying husband's atrophied leg (and her own spiritual conversion). On the night before he died from amyotrophic lateral sclerosis, his leg was restored to normal health. It happened at San Luis Rey Mission in California, and was witnessed by Father Joe Scerbo, Sister Betty Igo, and Father Ralph Weishaar. Her husband was a man of strong, unshakable faith, while hers was weak. But that has now changed. As Doris says, "Now, nothing will ever cause me to doubt again. I think this miracle was for me more than for my afflicted husband."

If Lillian C. of Alhambra, California, were asked, she would point to her friend who was miraculously healed of skin cancer. If Christian G. of Miami, Florida, were asked, he would point to his own radical deliverance from cocaine addiction. If Aminta Valls of Miami, Florida were asked, she would point to the miraculous disappearance of her daughter's brain tumor. If Ann Hussey of Somerset, Massachusetts, were asked, she would point to a crippled hand that became straight during a healing service. If Tom H. of Lawrence, Massachusetts were asked, he would point to a child who had died of heart failure, and then was raised from the dead through the prayers of a missionary nurse, to the amazement of the attending doctor.

In Your Life. If someone were to ask you the question, "What is a miracle?" what personal illustration would you give? Consider that question as you read about the characteristics of miracles in the upcoming chapter.

KEY POINTS

- Our church is founded on a miracle—the resurrection of Christ.
- The belief in miracles is a part of official Catholic teaching.
- Miracles are produced by God in a religious context to draw people to faith.
- Miracles are dramatic answers to prayer, normally instantaneous, and beyond ordinary means.
- Miracles are charisms of the Holy Spirit flowing through Christians baptized in the Holy Spirit.
- Miracles are promised in Scripture, given in confirmation, and released through baptism in the Holy Spirit.
- Counterfeit miracles can occur in an environment in which people are seeking power apart from God.
- As we allow the Holy Spirit to flow through us, he uses our identity in much the same way that electricity uses the filament in a light bulb.
- The miraculous work of God is much more common in our lives than we realize.

PRAYER

Spirit of understanding, what is a miracle? Give us your definition. Stir our minds and hearts to great heights as we consider the child raised from the dead, the car careening off the cliff, healing through holy water, the child in the womb, healing of brain tumors, skin cancer, crippled hands, and release from cocaine addiction. Bring us to deeper surrender and greater expectancy that you will do even greater things in and through us.

Lord, your whole church needs to believe in miracles again, as they did in the early days. Stir us up, Lord. Open us up, all of us, to the gift of endless possibilities in you. In Jesus' name. Amen.

THREE

Characteristics of Miracles

[The Church needs] The Spirit, the Holy Spirit, the anima-
tor and sanctifier... her divine breath... her unifying prin-
ciple, her inner source of light and strength, her support
and consoler, her source of charisms... **Pope Paul VI**[1]

He is Lord. Scripture is filled with a rich variety of miracle
stories, from Genesis to Revelation. Each story holds many
lessons, and is worth hours of reflection. Daniel's miraculous
protection in the lions' den (Daniel 6:22) reminds us that
Jesus is Lord over those who would destroy us. The fallen
walls of Jericho (Joshua 6) call us to remember that Jesus is
Lord over the obstacles in our lives.

The New Testament stories of miraculous deliverance
from demons remind us that Jesus is mightier than the powers of darkness (Ephesians 6:12). The stories of Lazarus (John
11:43-44) and Jairus' daughter (Mark 5:35-43) remind us of
his mastery over death. The stories of the miraculous multiplication of food (Mark 6:41), the calming of the storm (Mark
4:39), and walking on water (Mark 6:48-49) remind us of his
mastery over nature.

The stories of miraculous physical healings invite us to acknowledge Christ's lordship over our bodies. Most of the

miracles in the New Testament, and those which have occurred throughout the years, concern God's action on people's physical bodies. He is intimately concerned with our withered arms, our blind eyes, deaf ears, cancer, heart disease, arthritis, and every manner of illness. He is more than concerned; every infirmity is subject to his authority.

Miracles cover the full spectrum of human experience: finances, physical resources, health, marriage and family, relationships, emotions, addictions, personal habits. Nothing is beyond his reach; Jesus is Lord of all.

Tailor-Made. He brings miracles in as many ways as there are people, tailoring them to individual needs. To the fatherless, his miracle may point to "Abba." To the lonely, the abandoned, the bereaved, and the broken, his miracle will reveal his tender, compassionate heart. Each miracle will say, "I know you well; I am here to be what you need."

Every authentic Christian miracle will point to the cross and the resurrection, beginning with the initial miracle of salvation and continuing through all the subsequent large and small miracles that form our personal miracle history. "I died," he says to each and every person, "that you may be free. Receive my gifts, large and small. They are uniquely designed just for you."

The Instrument. Miracles may occur through a person or persons as they function as conduits of miracle power (recall the example of the electric light bulb). Sometimes Jesus gets directly involved, as in the following story by Molly M. of Stockton, California.

He Came into the Operating Room. "I was in the operating room having a heart catheterization for four heart blocks. I lay on the table stripped naked, and afraid, while the doctors and nurses were busy in the room. I cried out to Jesus, 'Help me!' The next thing I knew I felt a sense of peace. I looked down at the floor to my right and saw two feet with dust and nail scars. I looked up and there was Jesus standing beside me. He said, with great concern, 'I cried for you, my child, for I too was naked in front of my people.' I felt peace come, and knew that no matter what happened, he was with me. Then he told me I did not have what the doctors expected, but rather I had trouble in the left ventricular area of the heart. This was later verified by the doctors."

BASIC ELEMENTS COMMON TO ALL MIRACLES

Let us look now at some basic elements and characteristics common to miracles:

1. To Christians they are religious *signs* that reveal God's power and confirm their faith. "Therefore the Lord himself will give you a sign..." (Isaiah 7:14).

2. They are *transcendent*, extending beyond the limits of ordinary experience. "... his understanding no one can fathom" (Isaiah 40:28).

3. They are *marvels*, causing wonder and capturing attention. "Declare his glory among the nations, his marvelous deeds among all peoples" (Psalm 96:3).

GENERAL CHARACTERISTICS OF MIRACLES

1. Spiritual nature. Affects the spirit of a person by increasing faith, hope, and charity. "Jesus had said to him, 'Your son will live.' So he and all his household believed" (John 4:53). They are intended to lead to surrender to God and a relationship with him.

2. Moral nature. Affects the conduct of a person and helps lead to conversion. "The Lord is righteous in all his ways and loving toward all he has made" (Psalm 145:17).

3. Generally occur in answer to prayer. "So I say to you: Ask and it will be given to you; seek and you will find; knock and the door will be opened to you" (Luke 11:9).

4. Frequently occur in front of witnesses. "Some men came, bringing to him a paralytic.... He said to the paralytic, 'I tell you, get up, take your mat and go home.' He got up, took his mat and walked out in full view of them all. This amazed everyone and they praised God, saying 'We have never seen anything like this!'" (Mark 2:3,10-12).

5. Not necessarily dependent upon the faith of the individual receiving the miracle. An example might be the crippled beggar at the temple gate. He asked for money, but Peter said instead, "'... Silver or gold I do not have, but what I have I give you. In the name of Jesus Christ of Nazareth, walk.' Taking him by the right hand, he helped him up, and instantly the man's feet and ankles became strong. He jumped to his feet and began to walk...'" (Acts 3:6-8). For the beggar, faith apparently came after the miracle. God's action on his behalf captured his heart.

6. Promotes welfare. "A man with leprosy came to him and begged him on his knees, 'If you are willing, you can make me clean.' Filled with compassion, Jesus reached out his hand and touched the man. 'I am willing,' he said. 'Be clean!' Immediately the leprosy left him and he was cured" (Mark 1:40-42). Another example would be the woman with the issue of blood (Luke 8:43). Both of these people were untouchable under Jewish law; both reached out to Jesus and were accepted unconditionally. Their healing prepared them to reenter normal human life.

The following stories contain many of the characteristics common to miracles:

Never the Same. "I had been suffering from a hiatal hernia for about three years. The doctor put me on medication and told me never to eat in the evenings and always to sleep with my head raised. He said there was no other help available. About one month after the doctor put me on medication, I made a five-day retreat in California. On the fifth day during evening praise, three people laid hands on me and prayed for healing. I was instantly healed of the hernia and came to know the Lord as my personal Savior. I have never been the same since. I found myself no longer able to continue teaching biology; I had to teach God's Word. I now minister on an Indian reservation" (Sr. Veronica Fasbender, McLaughlin, South Dakota).

He Now Believes. "My husband was diagnosed as having a large acoustic neuroma, a tumor on the eighth cranial nerve affecting the hearing. It had grown into the brain stem. The doctor said my husband would probably die in surgery or, at best, come out with some kind of paralysis. Hundreds of people prayed before and during surgery. After twelve hours of surgery he was perfectly well, up and around the next day, and back to work in four weeks, rather than the predicted eight to ten weeks if all went well. My husband now believes in the power of God!" (Lucie Consentino, Methuen, Massachusetts).

BASIC TYPES OF PHYSICAL MIRACLES

In my work in the healing ministry I have seen all kinds of physical miracles. They can generally be placed in three basic groups:

1. An Essential Miracle. An example would be that of a

child who is missing an essential part of his eye. Scientists say he cannot read without that necessary part, and yet after prayer he is unexplainably able to read, even though the essential part is still missing.

2. A Miracle Regarding Mode. Nature can heal backs over a period of time. When one thousand people pray and thirty people are healed in a minute, however, we are encountering a mode, or method, that is above the power of nature.

3. Miracle Regarding Subject. For example, one would expect a man to lift fifty pounds, but if a three-year-old child did the same thing, then he would be acting beyond his capacities. This would be a miracle regarding the subject.

Sometimes people who cannot read will pray and then can read the Bible, and only the Bible. That is a miracle regarding subject.

TEN BASIC GROUPS

Let's examine miracles in various categories. I find it helpful to divide them by size into dramatic (small), more dramatic (medium), and most dramatic (large); and by type into physical, psychological, and spiritual. Many miracles will belong in more than one category, of course. A physical miracle can bring extraordinary spiritual healing, and vice versa. A psychological miracle can have dramatic effects in the physical and spiritual realm.

Physical miracles are those having reference primarily to material things. It might relate to the movement of a physical article, an action on a person's body, or even the running of a car for a period without the normal use of gasoline (as a number of people have experienced).

1. Dramatic (small) Physical Miracle. A woman told me a story one time about her son's lost wallet. They prayed and prayed and searched everywhere. Two days later he walked into his room and there on the table in front of him was his wallet.

In another situation, a man went to a prayer team requesting prayer for a persistent sinus condition. Medication had not improved the condition. After the prayer team members laid hands on the man, the sinus condition cleared up. These are dramatic (small) physical miracles.

2. More Dramatic (medium) Physical Miracle. Late one evening two teenage sisters left a shopping mall and headed for their car. It was dark and silent in the near-empty parking facility, and they were nervous. When they opened the car doors two men jumped out at them from behind the car, shouting, "You're not going anywhere! You're going with us!" The girls screamed and locked themselves in the car. The driver turned on the ignition and nothing happened. She tried again. No response. The men tried the doors. The girls joined hands and the driver prayed, "Dear God, please give us a miracle!" She turned on the ignition again and the motor started. She shifted into gear and raced out of the parking lot, leaving the men behind.

Safe at home, the girls told their father about the frightening experience. "I'm glad you're safe. That's the main thing. But don't stay out so late again." Then he reflected for an instant. "The car has never failed to start before. I'll check it out tomorrow." The next morning he raised the car's hood to examine the starter and saw something that raised gooseflesh on his arms: There was no battery!

Jane Kruse of Hartington, Nebraska, tells this story: "The most dramatic miracle I ever heard about happened to my son Timmy. In February, 1978, a few hours after he was born, he started to show signs of a heart problem. He started to turn blue. Our family doctor and three other doctors suggested we take him to a pediatric cardiologist in Omaha. The day we left, one of the doctors (who didn't want us to get our hopes up) told us to be prepared for the worst.

"In the meantime, when we first found out he might have a problem we asked Sister Stephanie Weber of Yankton, South Dakota, and a few other friends to pray for Timmy's healing. Then on the day we left for Omaha we stopped at Sacred Heart Convent in Yankton, South Dakota, to ask Sister Rosemary Ford, O.S.B., for prayer. When we left she told us to bring back the good news. Her optimism stayed in our minds.

"During our five-day stay in Omaha the doctors ran all kinds of tests. All came back normal; some were even better than normal. I'll never forget when the doctor asked, 'Why did you bring him to me? He is the healthiest baby I have ever seen. There's nothing wrong with him.' My husband and I said ecstatically, 'It's a miracle!' The doctor replied, 'Yes, I guess it must be.'"

This story of a cancer patient is told by Dr. Richard Eby in *Caught up into Paradise*. Tests revealed a very large pelvic tumor, but in the operating room they discovered an invasive metastasized carcinoma involving gut, bladder, and pelvic walls. The doctors scooped out handfuls of bloody disintegrating tissue, half filling a bucket, and then closed the incision in grim silence.

The following morning when Dr. Eby visited the patient, she was bright, alive, and well. Her family explained how her church friends had simply prayed for her recovery after surgery, and expected it to happen.

Fifteen years later Dr. Eby saw this woman again, healthy and well. Only Jesus knows how many lives were changed through her healing.

3. Most Dramatic (large) Physical Miracle. Brenda Stillwell of Ontario, Canada, shared Noah's miracle: "When I first saw Noah, he was a severely retarded ten-month-old baby in an orphanage in Haiti. He would lie all day with his tongue hanging out, never sitting up and never rolling over. When an infant flu swept through the orphanage, Noah became very ill and died. Some friends told me that as his body was cooling, two volunteers were in the next room praying for him. They prayed (not knowing he had already died), 'Lord, you made Noah. He is your child, and you have a plan for his life. We place him in your hands in trust. Thank you, Lord. Amen.' Ten minutes later someone approached the women and said, 'Noah just finished his bottle and wants another.' In the days and weeks to follow it became evident that Noah was no longer mentally retarded; he was a normal child. He did things a little differently, however. For example, he learned to stand before he learned to sit."

Consider another story from Dr. Richard Eby's experience. Early in his practice he had delivered a husky eight-pound baby boy, and then left to meet a patient at another hospital. Thirty minutes later he received word that the baby had stopped breathing. Resuscitation procedures began while he raced back to the hospital, praying for Jesus to revive the body. When he arrived (fifty minutes after the baby died), rescue team members shook their heads and assured him they had done everything possible. Dr. Eby laid his hand on the baby's cold head and prayed, "Dear Jesus, he was so loved down here. Won't you give him back to us? His mother needs him, just like my mother needed me." The body began to cough and convulse. Then the baby began to scream.

Medical books say that eight minutes without breathing is fatal for an infant's brain tissue. On the way home Dr. Eby prayed, "Please give that baby a new brain, undamaged and unhampered by these long minutes of death." The Lord answered that prayer. Sixteen years later the local paper carried a story about the captain of the football team. It was Dr. Eby's "baby," scholastically and physically a winner.

Father John H. Hampsch, C.M.F., of Los Angeles, California, reported some amazing events in the miracle survey. During his international travels in a teaching and healing ministry, he has seen or received reports of: resuscitation miracles (several); restoration of limbs missing from thalidomide-caused deformities (within twenty minutes); and a restored breast, overnight, from a mastectomy.

4. Dramatic (small) Psychological Miracle. Psychological miracles are dramatic answers to prayer by which there is healing on a psychological level, such as instantaneous healing of a year of depression which doctors had not been able to cure. Consider this story from Phyllis C. of South Dakota: "I came to believe in miracles when I was baptized in the Holy Spirit on a Cursillo weekend. At that time Jesus healed the psychological pain caused by my difficult fourteen years of marriage. He led me step by step through each year of pain, rejection, lack of communication, and lack of love. As he recalled year 14, 13, 12, 11, etc., he said to me, 'Phyllis, I was there....' He healed and healed and healed back to our wedding day. I became a new person with strength to carry on."

5. More Dramatic (medium) Psychological Miracle. A woman in a Latin American country was crippled in an automobile accident when her sister was driving. For fifteen years she hated God and her sister. At a prayer meeting she was set totally free from the negativity and became one of the most active participants in the charismatic renewal in her country.

Andy Pangelina from San Jose, California, tells how forgiveness opened the door to a miracle in his life: "My mother died when I was born, and my father died of alcoholism when I was about twenty years old. I was passed around from relative to relative until I was seventeen, when I first went to jail. I got into drugs and alcohol and ran with a gang in southern California.

"When I was nineteen and my fiancee was killed in an auto accident, I became bitter and angry. I've been in jails across the United States and was at one time a major drug dealer in northern California.

"It was my sons, my daughter, and my wife who eventually brought me to the Lord. I tried to accept the Lord many times over the years, but it didn't seem to make any difference. The first real change came when I was in a mental hospital. My daughter wrote me a note, asking forgiveness for the time she told me to move out of our home. With all the things I had done to her, she came to *me* asking for forgiveness! It really got to me. I began feeling a lot of support from my family. My wife and kids prayed for me and loved me and cared about me. I really began seeking the Lord at that time, and could feel a deep internal change.

"Some people from the Christ the King prayer community in San Jose, California, prayed over me, and I could feel the Lord Jesus finally beginning to take over. That was in 1979. Today I am involved in prayer group leadership and coordinate the 'Wounded Healer' ministry to substance abusers in our area. We have a weekly prayer meeting and various outreaches to ex-prisoners, families of prisoners, ex-drug addicts and alcoholics."

6. Most Dramatic (large) Psychological Miracle. The work of Dr. Kenneth McAll, a psychiatrist in England, is most extraordinary. Dr. McAll practiced medicine in China after he obtained his degree from Edinburgh University. His experiences in China led to interest in the powers of possession, and he has devoted his life since to the curing of psychiatric illness through divine guidance. He has practiced as a consultant psychiatrist in England for twenty-five years and is an associate member of the Royal College of Psychiatrists.

We learn from Dr. McAll that as negative ties are cut between the living and the dead through Eucharistic services, people are set free from many physical and emotional illnesses classified as hopeless. Even schizophrenics have been reportedly healed through this process. Some of my experiences in freeing people from negative attachments to the past are recorded in my book, *Intergenerational Healing.*[2]

7. Spiritual Miracles. In almost every "Life in the Spirit" seminar, people are transformed. Alcoholics, drug addicts, agnostics, and atheists have been healed and converted in these seminars. In fact, when I conduct healing services I try to be sure that everyone is baptized in the Spirit (and praying in tongues) early in the session. This process of surrender opens the door to miracles. A representative of the archdiocese of New York said one time that the Hispanic Catholic charismatic renewal is the best tool for evangelization of drug addicts, prostitutes, and alcoholics. They are often instantly healed in such a spiritually powerful environment. Jim H. of Stayton, Oregon, shared in the survey about a man who drank a fifth of whiskey a day; he was totally healed at a "Life in the Spirit" seminar.

8. Dramatic (small) Spiritual Miracle. The late Father Joe Diebels of San Francisco, California, shared his story in my book, *Coming to Life:* "The first time I went to a prayer meeting I hid in the back against the wall and hoped no one would recognize me. I was negative about the need for being baptized in the Holy Spirit because I figured, 'Why should I have hands laid on me? I'm a priest, and I have the Holy Spirit.' Then after observing the people I thought, 'These people are believing that Jesus is right here.' At that point it occurred to me that I had a problem. I was humbled, and deeply moved. I said, 'Lord, I wish You would really be here when I pray.' As soon as I expressed this desire, I felt His presence right beside me. That changed things for me. I began to attend meetings regularly and went through a 'Life in the Spirit' seminar. After being baptized in the Spirit, my work in campus ministry greatly improved. Students began to seek me out regularly. In a conversation with my archbishop I was asked how I was different since being baptized in the Holy Spirit. I replied, 'The difference is that now, what I do—works!'"[3]

9. More Dramatic (medium) Spiritual Miracle. Marilynn Kramar, a Catholic lay evangelist with the Hispanic communities in Los Angeles, California, has a fascinating conversion story. As the wife of an Assemblies of God minister, she set out to convert the nuns across the street. They invited her to come to Mass with them. She came, intending to convert them, and was herself converted to Catholicism. Today she is one of the leading Catholic evangelists in the United States.

10. Most Dramatic (large) Spiritual Miracle. In Scripture, the conversion of Paul (Acts 9:3) is an example of a most dramatic spiritual miracle. The story of Father Leonardo Polinar, a village priest from the Philippines, is another example. In his work with the poor he became indoctrinated with Communism and eventually joined the Communist guerrillas. He was caught and brought to a military camp. When he was released Fe Baluyot, a friend of his mother, took him to a prayer meeting in a nearby city. A team prayed over him and he left, turned off by the experience. He went back to the hills, was caught again, released again, and taken again by Fe to the prayer meeting. This time he saw a different light. His heart was softened. When he sat down for prayer he began to cry. He recommitted his life to the Lord Jesus Christ, was baptized in the Holy Spirit, and radically converted. He now goes around the world in a powerful healing ministry.

TO REVIEW:

DRAMATIC	MORE DRAMATIC	MOST DRAMATIC
PHYSICAL	PHYSICAL	PHYSICAL
1. man's sinus problem 2. lost wallet	1. teenage girls' battery 2. Timmy's heart 3. woman's cancer	1. Noah's resuscitation 2. Fr. Hampsch's stories of restored body parts
PSYCHOLOGICAL	PSYCHOLOGICAL	PSYCHOLOGICAL
Phyllis' marriage	Andy's and Latin American woman's forgiveness	1. work of Dr. McAll 2. Marianne's mental illness
SPIRITUAL	SPIRITUAL	SPIRITUAL
Fr. Joe's ministry empowerment	Marilynn Kramar's conversion	Fr. Polinar's radical conversion

Inside the Gift. Whether a miracle involves a lost wallet, driving without a battery, spiritual conversion, or a baby restored to life, the message from the Lord rings loud and clear: "I am here to help you and to stir up your faith. I care about you and the things that concern you. Yield to me. Receive the help I am offering." The miracles in our lives point to the deep personal commitment the Lord has made to us, and call us to a deep personal commitment to him. They also teach us about covenant, which we will discuss in the next chapter.

KEY POINTS

- The miracles in Scripture invite us to acknowledge the lordship of Jesus over the power of darkness, death, nature, and physical bodies.
- His miracles are tailor-made to the nature and need of every person.
- All authentic Christian miracles point to the death and resurrection of Jesus Christ.
- Miracles may occur through an intermediary or through the direct action of Jesus without an intermediary.
- Miracles are religious *signs;* they are *transcendent;* and they are *marvels.*
- Miracles have *spiritual* and *moral* dimensions; they generally are *answers to prayer;* they usually occur in front of *witnesses;* they *do not necessarily depend on the faith* of the recipient; and they *promote the welfare of people.*
- There are *essential* miracles, miracles of *mode,* and miracles of *subject.*
- Miracles fall into basic groupings of *physical, psychological,* and *spiritual.*
- The message behind the miracles is that the Lord desires to help us, and to form a relationship with us.

PRAYER

Come, Spirit of counsel, and teach us through the experiences of Daniel and Lazarus; through baby Noah, Father Joe, and Sister Veronica; through missing batteries and Andy's daughter; through Timmy, the metastasized cancer, and all the other stories. Fill in the gaps between those things we have learned about miracles and those things you want us to know. In Jesus' name. Amen.

FOUR

Miracle Covenants

The Church lives on the Holy Spirit. The Church was truly born, you could say, on the day of Pentecost. The Church's first need is always to live Pentecost.... **Pope Paul VI[1]**

He Stopped in Midair. Doris from California told a story about a construction worker who fell from a scaffolding several stories above the ground. As he fell he cried, "Oh, God!" He suddenly stopped in midair, giving him time to grab the edge of the platform and save himself. His coworkers, observing the amazing midair suspension, carefully avoided him for days after the occurrence.

Some people fear God, and shy away from manifestations of his power. Those who have never had a personal experience of his love—having only an intellectual knowledge of him as creator, first mover, alpha and omega—may be shocked by physical manifestations of his presence. They may not know what to do with the idea that God would actually step in and give specific help in a direct, personal way.

The purpose of this chapter is make the reader more aware of the Lord's covenant promises to give specific, practical help. Our covenant heritage is far greater than many understand.

The Most Important Verse in the Bible. Often in my services I will ask, "What is the most important verse in the Bible?" People in the congregation will raise their hands and suggest various verses. I will thank them and continue asking, until that rare person calls out, "God is love." "And so we know and rely on the love God has for us. God is love. Whoever lives in love lives in God, and God in him" (1 John 4:16).

Why Is It Important? This verse describes the nature of God. Everyone searches for love. It's a universal need in every age and every culture. More than anything else, we need to know that there is someone who understands us completely and loves us unconditionally. We spend our lives looking for love. At various times we think we have found it, yet sooner or later we are disappointed. Only God can perfectly satisfy that place in our hearts, because we were created to love him and be loved by him. When we meet and surrender to his love we are, for the first time, complete inside ourselves.

Loving Is Giving. Love by its nature has to give. There is an old familiar saying, "Love isn't love until it's given away." To love is to give. The world says "Take!" God says "Give!"

Matthew 7:11 says, "If you, then, though you are evil, know how to give good gifts to your children, how much more will your Father in heaven give good gifts to those who ask him!" Look at the way you, parents, give to your children. You live for them and deprive yourselves for them. Yet the love you have for your children is only a faint reflection of the love of your heavenly Father for you.

Covenant Love. God has been working in people's hearts for thousands of years, to draw them into a knowledge of this love that longs to give. This teaching is beautifully illustrated in his covenant with Abraham (Genesis 15), who came from a region in Mesopotamia where people worshiped the moon god, Sin, and knew nothing of a God who wanted to give.

Historically, Jewish people understand covenant better than other people do. From the third millennium on, there were many evidences of covenant in Jewish and non-Jewish cultures. It was understood to be an ordinary way of entering into contract.

Since Vatican II, however, there has been a renewed appreciation of the meaning of covenant in our Catholic heritage. The better we understand covenant, the more we will appreciate how our heavenly Father is committed to help us. We will see how much he is *for* us, and not *against* us.

The common Hebrew word for covenant is *berth*. According to *Covenant in the Old Testament* by Michael D. Guinan, O.F.M., a covenant is "...an agreement or promise between two parties, solemnly professed before witnesses and made binding by an oath expressed verbally or by some symbolic action." From a theological standpoint, a covenant is one undertaken by God for the benefit of those who receive the promises by faith and make a personal commitment to him.

Most are called "blood" covenants because of the element of sacrifice. The Old Testament term "cutting a covenant" is derived from this sacrificial action. The covenant is generally sealed through a ritual which includes sacrificing an animal (such as a calf) and splitting it head to tail. Covenant representatives walked between the halves of a slain animal and pronounced a curse upon those who had violated the pact.

The development and renewal of covenant relationships throughout the Old Testament is a constant reminder of God's desire to give to his people. "He gives... He gives... He gives...." These words are found hundreds of times throughout Scripture, reminding us over and over that the Lord wants to give his people good things.

God promised Abraham a son, and descendants as many as the stars in the sky, and he proved his intentions through the covenant process familiar to Abraham. This settled for Abraham that it was truly God's will for him to receive all that God had to give. When God then asked Abraham to sacrifice his son Isaac, Abraham gave him freely. Isaac already belonged to God.

When Abraham placed his son on the altar, his action foreshadowed God's gift of his own Son on the altar of the cross. "He who did not spare his own Son, but gave him up for us all—how will he not also, along with him, graciously give us all things?" (Romans 8:32).

The *Documents of Vatican II* state: "In carefully planning and preparing the salvation of the whole human race, the God of supreme love... chose for Himself a person to whom He might entrust His promise. First He entered into a covenant with Abraham (Genesis 18:18) and, through Moses, with the people of Israel (Exodus 24:8)...."[2]

The New Covenant. At Calvary, Jesus became the sacrifice of the New Covenant. He rose again to become our covenant representative; that is, to stand in for us before his Father. He gave himself as our covenant meal. Jesus has exchanged his strength for our weakness, his supply for our need, his health for our sickness. He gave us his name, his authority, his armor, and his weapons.

Through Jesus we enter into a covenant with our heavenly Father and become adopted sons and daughters of God. "...but you received the Spirit of sonship. And by him we cry, 'Abba, Father.' The Spirit himself testifies with our spirit that we are God's children. Now if we are children, then we are heirs—heirs of God and co-heirs with Christ..." (Romans 8:15-17). Jesus told people he could do extraordinary things because he was related to the Father, and that through him they, too, could be related to the Father and do extraordinary things. "His divine power has given us everything we need for life and godliness through our knowledge of him who called us by his own glory and goodness. Through these he has given us his very great and precious promises, so that

through them you may participate in the divine nature..."
(2 Peter 1:3-4).

In the following stories Linda, Diana, and Elizabeth share family memories of covenant love.

Dad's Miracle. "My Dutch father, Charlie, was an atheist all of his life, and the son of an atheist. My mother, sister, and I had prayed for his conversion for years, asking the Lord to keep him alive until he accepted Jesus. One time when Dad was very ill an angel came and stood beside him. Dad saw the angel and cried out, 'No! I'm not ready to go.' The angel left.

"Some months later he was confined to bed, paralyzed and close to death. One afternoon he cried out, 'I need help!' Mom tried to assist with physical needs but he said 'No, you don't understand! I need *help!*' When my sister arrived and knelt beside his bed, he accepted the Lord Jesus Christ. In the weeks to follow we stood back and quietly watched his miraculous recovery. He began to move; he could sit up; he walked; he functioned normally for an eighty-year-old man.

"For five years the Holy Spirit ministered to my father, holding him safe, bringing reconciliation, forgiveness, and love. At the end of five years when Dad was comfortable about going to his new home, he died a peaceful, gentle death.

"When I think about covenant, I think about what the Lord did for my dad" (Linda Schubert, Sunnyvale, California).

The Miracle of the Toys and Bibles. "When I was nine years old our family lived near Cincinnati, Ohio, in a valley by a creek that flowed into the Little Miami River. The oldest of five children, I was often left in charge when my parents went out for their traditional evening walk through the woods and along the creek.

"One Saturday night when they were out walking, it occurred to me to have each of my brothers and sisters gather up all their toys and put them in a pile under our buckeye tree. I collected mine and put them with their toys. When my parents came back I was in trouble for breaking the family rules, but it was too late to return the toys to the house, except for one quick load. I promised to bring them in after church the next day.

"When we were driving down the hill to our house after church, we saw smoke rising from our property. Our house was on fire. We huddled together in shock and watched it become engulfed in flames. The fire was so hot that even the food in the refrigerator was cooked.

"A number of days later Mom and Dad began picking through the ruins to see if anything had survived the fire. What they discovered is still a matter of conversation in our family, more than thirty years later.

"My father had always loved the Bible. Perhaps that love came from my great-grandmother, who used to hold me on her lap in the big rocking chair and read Bible stories. She died several months before the fire, leaving her treasured family Bible with my dad. We had, in fact, seven Bibles in various parts of the house. Every Bible survived the fire, which destroyed almost everything else.

"The Lord saved almost all the children's toys and all the family Bibles: the toys through prompting me to do something that made no sense, and the Bibles through a direct action in the midst of a 'fiery furnace.' His protection of the beloved Bibles gave the family a deep sense of trust in the midst of desolation. It was like the Lord was saying, 'Stay focused on me. Keep your eyes on me, not on your circumstances. I will carry you through.' 'So we fix our eyes not on what is seen, but on what is unseen. For what is seen is temporary, but what is unseen is eternal'" (2 Corinthians 4:18) (Diana Gopal, Sunnyvale, California).

His Protective Care. "In 1937 I lived high on a 2500-acre mountaintop ranch on the California coast. The road to the ranch was winding and steep, a narrow ribbon cut into the edge of the rugged mountain. I was nine months pregnant with my second child, and very large. Castor oil, quinine, and rides on the rough road did not promote delivery. My regular doctor was 400 miles away in Los Angeles, and the local doctor did not realize that my birth channel was not adequate for a large baby.

"That period is as vivid in my mind today as it was all those years ago. The Lord's miraculous protection of my child and myself brought a peace I cannot begin to adequately describe. As I waited there on the mountain I could see in my spirit heavenly white particles covering me. I knew we were safe; I knew we were in his warm, protective care.

"When the tenth month arrived, my husband contacted our Los Angeles physician and we made the decision to drive south. Highway One, which had just been completed between Carmel and Los Angeles, was a narrow, winding coast road with a steep cliff down to the Pacific Ocean. As we bounced along in our little 1930s Ford, I held my hands over my baby in the womb and thanked the Lord for his supernatural protection of our lives—my child's and mine.

"At the hospital the Lord provided a good night's rest and an early morning caesarean delivery of a healthy, thirteen-pound girl. 'Though the mountains be shaken and the hills be removed, yet my unfailing love for you will not be shaken nor my covenant of peace be removed,' says the Lord, who has compassion on you'" (Isaiah 54:10). (Elizabeth Vander Ploeg, Oregon)

KEY POINTS

- To understand covenant we must first believe that God is a loving Father who wants to give and to bless.
- God's covenant with Abraham carved a path to the cross of Jesus Christ.
- Jesus' surrender fulfilled the covenant, extending it to all people in every age.
- Vatican II brought renewed appreciation of our covenant heritage.
- Jesus did extraordinary things because he was related to the Father.
- Through Jesus we can have a relationship with the Father and do extraordinary things.
- Received in faith, Jesus is our strength in weakness, our health in sickness.

PRAYER

Come, Spirit of love, and plant deep in our hearts a knowledge of God as loving Father. Please work out in our daily lives the implications of your covenant, which has its roots in your covenant with Abraham. You have conquered our death and given us new life, filled with grace and power. You are our strength, our health, our victory. Come, Spirit of love, and open our spiritual eyes, that we may see your miraculous, ongoing work in our lives. In Jesus' name. Amen.

FIVE

Miracles through the Centuries

The Church needs her perennial Pentecost; she needs fire in the heart, words on the lips, prophecy in the glance. The Church needs to be the temple of the Holy Spirit....

Pope Paul VI[1]

Uncounted Miracles. From the time of the apostles to the present day, there have been people through whom Jesus has poured out his power. Miracles have generally flowed most freely through those friends of Jesus most concerned with the downtrodden, the poor, and the needy. Some of these "coworkers with the Lord" will be briefly introduced in this section. While we can only glimpse at a few of them through the following quotations, it will help us to gain a sense of the flow of miracles in our heritage.

A FEW MORE MIRACLE WORKERS OF THE CHURCH[2]

Healing Grace. St. Irenaeus (120-202): "Christ's true disciples having received grace from Him use it for the benefit of the rest of humanity, even as each has received the gift from

Him. For some drive out demons... some have foreknowledge of things to be... others cure the sick... the dead have been raised...."

Gifts for Everyone. Tertullian (d. 225): "We... regard the rest of the powers of the Holy Spirit as tools of the Church to whom the Spirit was sent, administering all of the outstandingly impressive gifts to everyone just as the Lord distributes to each."

A Matter of Willingness. St. Hilary of Poitiers (d. 367): "So the human mind, unless it has by faith appropriated the gifts of the Holy Spirit, will have the natural faculty of apprehending God, but it will not have the light of knowledge. That gift, which is in Christ, is available to all alike: it is nowhere withheld, but is given to each in proportion to his willingness to be worthy of it. The gifts of the Spirit continue with us to the final consummation of history; this is the solace of our waiting; in the working of His gifts is the pledge of our hope for the future, the light of our minds, the radiance shed on our hearts."

Holy Spirit Brings Miracles. St. Basil the Great (d. 379): "The Spirit is ever present with those who are worthy, but works, as need requires, in prophecies or in healings or in some other actual carrying into effect of His miraculous power."

Nearly Seventy Recorded. St. Augustine of Hippo (354-430): "Once I realized how many miracles were occurring in our own day and which were so like the miracles of old and also how wrong it would be to allow the memory of these marvels of divine power to perish from among our people, I recorded them. It is only two years ago that the keeping of records was begun here in Hippo, and already, at this writing, we have nearly seventy attested miracles. I know with certain knowledge of many others which have not, so far, been officially recorded."

Power and Humility. Pope Gregory the Great (540-604): "The soul that is really filled with the Spirit of God will easily be recognized by its miraculous powers and humility."

Faith and Relics. St. John Damascene (d. 749) spoke of miraculous powers of relics, and the miracles that took place because the common people had the gift of supernatural faith.

The Grace of Faith. St. Symeon The New Theologian (949-1022): "In fact, all knowledge and all discernment, every word of wisdom and every word of a more mystical knowledge and also the power of miracles and the gift of prophecy, divers tongues and their interpretation... the discernment of future goods and the acquisition of the Kingdom of Heaven... in a word, all that unbelievers fail to know and that we, after having received the grace of faith, can know, think, and say, all this comes uniquely from the teaching of the Spirit."

Padre Pio, Sister Briege, and the Rest of Us. The Holy Spirit has persistently revealed Jesus through signs and wonders throughout the centuries and in recent times. Padre Pio Forgione (1887-1968) was a Capuchin monk who manifested the charismatic gifts of wisdom, knowledge, discernment, and healing. A survey respondent shared about a woman who had a disease which caused irreversible hemorrhaging; her doctor sent her home to die. A priest friend brought her Padre Pio's rosary, placed it on her, and prayed. She was totally healed.

In the 1920s to 1950s, the Holy Spirit flowed powerfully through Father Solanus Casey, O.F.M. (1871-1957) of Chicago. It is said that the majority of the people he prayed for were healed. Amazing miracles are occurring as the Holy Spirit flows through Father Ralph DiOrio of Massachusetts and Father Edward McDonough of Massachusetts. Miraculous cures of cancer happen in the ministry of Sister Briege McKenna, O.S.C., of Florida. Father Emilien Tardif was dying of acute pulmonary tuberculosis in his native Canada when the Lord miraculously healed him. His book *Jesus is Alive*[3] recounts many of the miracles in his international ministry. Father Rick Thomas recounts many miracles with the poor in *Miracles in El Paso?*[4]

These are only a few whom the Lord has raised up as models. In every diocese, in every state, in every country the Spirit of Jesus is pouring his miracle power through priests and religious, hospital employees, bankers, police officers, secretaries, dock workers, and lawyers. He equips for service every willing person from every walk of life. The gifts and graces that have been manifested throughout the ages are the same gifts and graces poured out by the Holy Spirit at Pentecost for the purpose of building and strengthening the Body of Christ.

KEY POINTS

- Miracles generally flow most freely through those persons who are deeply concerned with the needy.
- The church fathers remind us of the importance of our willingness to be used.
- The presence of power and humility are characteristics of the coworkers of Jesus.
- Vatican II reminds us that charisms of the Holy Spirit are to be received with grateful appreciation for their help to the church.
- Through the ages there have been visible and hidden models of the miracle ministry of the church.

PRAYER

Come, Spirit of faithfulness, and form us into a new generation of saints, deeply surrendered and filled with great expectation. Permeate us with the grace and power of Pentecost. Help us to become faithful coworkers in miracles with you. Come, Spirit of faithfulness. In Jesus' name. Amen.

PART II

ENTERING IN

*"Come, you who are blessed by my Father;
take your inheritance...."* **Matthew 25:34**

SIX

Yielding—the Secret of Miracle Power

The Spirit who makes us Christians and raises us to supernatural life, is the true and profound principle of our interior life and of our external apostolic activity....

Pope Paul VI[1]

Give Your Hurts to Jesus. "I have never understood why mothers tell their children, 'Mommy will kiss it better,' " Betty Peissner of Pleasant Hill, California, reflected one day. "I knew I could never make anything better, but Jesus could. I always tell my kids, 'Give your hurts to Jesus.' When my daughter, Mary, was five years old she learned the power of surrender to Jesus in a crisis. She was hit by a car and knocked twenty-five feet. When I rushed outside I found her in a coma. I leaned over her unconscious body and whispered in her ear, 'Mary, did you give your hurt to Jesus?' She opened her eyes, looked at me and said, 'Yes, Mom, I did.' Then she lapsed back into the coma.

"The doctors at the hospital said she had broken ribs and a ruptured spleen. There would be three hours of surgery, and she might die.

"That's when the miracle happened. A short while after reaching the hospital Mary came out of her coma. Subsequent X-rays showed that the spleen had been miraculously welded together, as had her ribs. I was surprised, and the doctors were flabbergasted.

"That night when I was praising God he told me, 'I will direct your children's lives, not you. All you have to do is teach them to love me.'"

Love Invites Surrender. As love for the Lord begins to take root and grow, he invites us into deeper surrender and commitment. When people get married they say two little words, "I do," and their lives are forever changed. They have entered into a covenant, witnessed by the Lord Jesus Christ. Saying "I do" to Jesus begins our miracle journey with its covenant promises. Ongoing, deeper surrender draws us into baptism in the Holy Spirit, release of the gifts of the Spirit, and countless opportunities to grow in love through service. The greatest gift I can ask the Holy Spirit to give you is the ability to say "Yes" to him with your whole heart, mind, soul, and body.

A Work of the Holy Spirit. Our surrender to Jesus is orchestrated by the Holy Spirit who works through our ordinary circumstances at home, on the job, and at play. His objective is to bring his people into a place where Jesus is revealed in their lives. When Jesus is revealed, we begin living in the realm of the miraculous.

The Lord will do as much as we allow him to do. He says, "Give me your problems, your addictions, your pain. Let me be your victory." If we respond, "No, Lord, I have to do it my way," he will step aside and wait. He will never force; he respects our free will.

Through the enabling grace of the Holy Spirit, we "give all our hurts to Jesus," as did Mary in the earlier story. Whether the hurts are physical, psychological, or spiritual, they belong to him.

Sister Briege McKenna in *Miracles Do Happen* reminds us that when we "… can say yes to him, we will never be hurt. The Lord never does anything in our lives that will hurt us. He is a God of love. It is in our resistance and our pulling away and saying no that we actually hurt ourselves."[2]

We must come to the end of our resistance and open our spirits to him. Surrender is the only answer. Only in total surrender are we truly free. We can open ourselves and yield to his cleansing and healing work; we can't cleanse and heal ourselves.

As we sit with the Lord, little and alone and helpless and learning to trust, he fills us with himself. Deep yielding requires deep prayer. Resolve to spend quality time with him alone, in community and with a prayer partner.

Brenda Stillwell from Ontario, Canada, speaks of the Lord's patience with us in prayer: "The Lord in his gentleness and love is so patient with us. He is so faithful. If we just begin to pray and ask, even in the act of praying he gives us faith. Pray, 'Lord, I have no faith, but I'm praying anyway. Lord, I can't promise not to doubt, but I will keep on asking, knocking, and seeking. I won't stop.' In our seeking, the Lord is faithful. Keep going; keep trying to lay hold of him in prayer. Say, 'Lord, you want me to grow. Whatever lesson you want me to learn, I want to learn it.'"

I am personally committed to a minimum of three hours a day in prayer. Without that faithful commitment to the Lord I cannot accomplish the work set before me. In that time, which is not easy, the Lord continues to reveal areas in my life that need to be brought under his dominion.

The primary symbol of our faith is the cross, an instrument of execution, that continually reminds us of our utter powerlessness. "I have been crucified with Christ and I no longer live, but Christ lives in me. The life I live in the body, I live by faith in the Son of God, who loved me and gave himself for me" (Galatians 2:20).

A Battlefield. Asking for the gift of miracles is asking for assignment on the front lines of a battlefield. When we agree to go into the front lines for the Lord, we are going to face opposition. He tells us to "put on the full armor of God" because our struggle "... is not against flesh and blood, but against the rulers, against the authorities, against the powers of this dark world and against the spiritual forces of evil in the heavenly realms" (Ephesians 6:11-12). Spiritual warfare requires two actions: submitting to God and resisting the enemy (James 4:7).

He's Building a Home. The Holy Spirit will draw us in our powerlessness to believe in the face of the impossible; to hope when everyone says, "Don't get your hopes up"; to praise with an empty heart; and to thank him even when we don't see any results. He will call us to forgive the unforgivable, to speak when we have no courage, to act in spite of fear, to be silent when we would gossip or criticize, to fast when we are hungry, and to give money with a nearly empty bank account. He raises us up to display his power (Romans 9:17), calling us to an obedience that the world would not understand. In so doing, he is building a home for himself through which he can supply miracles to the hurting world.

KEY POINTS

- Love invites surrender.
- Saying "Yes" to Jesus begins our miracle journey.
- In our resistance we hurt ourselves.
- Yielding involves stepping aside and turning over control to the Holy Spirit, who reveals Jesus.
- Yielding involves a committed prayer time.
- There is a spiritual warfare element in a miracle ministry.

- He is building a home within us, from which to supply miracles to the world.
- The cross reminds us of our powerlessness.
- The resurrection reminds us of his power.

PRAYER

Come, Spirit of godliness, and strip away any pettiness, jealousy, or negative preoccupations that separate us from you. We let go of all areas of resistance. We stop fighting your way of doing things. We accept your will for our lives. Come, Spirit of godliness, and rule in our hearts. Melt us, mold us, fill us, use us. In Jesus' name. Amen.

SEVEN

Responding—Action Steps to Miracles

By possessing these charisms... there arises for each of the faithful both the right and duty to use them... for the well-being of mankind and growth of the Church. They are to be used in the freedom of the Spirit who "breathes wherever He wills" (John 3:8). They are to be used in mutual cooperation with all Christ's brothers, especially in cooperation with their pastors, whose duty it is to make judgment about the genuineness of these gifts and the disciplined use of them, not indeed "to extinguish the Spirit" (1 Thessalonians 5:19), but to "test all things and to hold on to that which is good" (1 Thessalonians 5:21).

Decree on the Apostolate of the Laity[1]

"Whom Shall I Send?" Evelyn LaBella of Portland, Oregon, was out walking her dog one day when she saw a neighbor waiting for a bus to take her to the hospital to visit Ben, her critically ill grandson. Evelyn knew instantly, with an inner certainty, that she was to go and pray for Ben. She dashed home, changed her clothes, drove to the hospital, and with the permission of relatives (who also joined her in prayer) she read some Scripture verses about healing and prayed for the boy to be totally healed. He had a miraculous recovery.

"Here Am I. Send Me". "Then I heard the voice of the Lord saying, 'Whom shall I send? And who will go for us?' And I said, 'Here am I. Send me!'" (Isaiah 6:8). In this chapter we will reflect upon some ways of answering his call when he says, "Whom shall I send?" I pray the Holy Spirit will give you a clear understanding of some of the ways he is personally calling you.

Every Available Person. A Pentecostal minister said to me one time when I was fairly new in the renewal, "God wants to heal his wounded people so much that he will use anyone." This was a life-changing message for me. I began to study the healing activity of the Holy Spirit from the earliest records to the present day in the charismatic renewal. In the hundreds of healing workshops I have subsequently conducted around the world, I have seen all the manifestation gifts of 1 Corinthians 12 evident in those individuals who opened their spirits and yielded. There is clear evidence that the Spirit of Jesus is eager to flow powerfully through every willing person.

Dorothea's Experience. My sister, Dorothea DeGrandis Sudol, learned this truth one time at a conference. She had motioned for me to come and pray for some people on the other side of the room. I said to her, "Dottie, you pray for them. I'm busy." A little surprised, she said, "I'm a lay person. I've never done that before." I responded, "Dottie, you are better than nothing." She stepped out in faith and prayed for the people who were waiting. The outcome was that they were blessed and so was she. Today she has her own international ministry. The Lord will use every willing person.

Where Do I Start? Mother Teresa of Calcutta tells a story of looking all over India, and then starting with the people in front of her. Her simple actions have affected not only India, but the entire world. The Lord tells us, "Heal the sick, raise the dead, cleanse those who have leprosy, drive out demons. Freely you have received, freely give" (Matthew 10:8). We start with the people in front of us. One might ask, "Why am I thinking of this person, or that one? Why am I preoccupied with this neighbor? Is there something the Lord would have me do?" Don't dismiss your preoccupation before checking it out with the Lord to see if there is some action he would have you take regarding that matter.

Yield, listen, and step out in faith. Act on what he says, and more will follow. Pray; allow the Spirit to flow. Something about a situation may "light up," such as the experience with Evelyn LaBella, the woman who prayed for Ben. There is an interior witness of the Spirit when the Lord says, "Go," or "Do."

Follow the Flow of Love. You might say, "I'm not sure if it is really God. I don't always hear him clearly." A rule of thumb some people use is this: Follow the flow of love. God is love, and as you yield to him, his miraculous love will flow through you. His love will pull you like a magnet to those he wants to bless, to touch, and to heal through you. Catholics have always believed in the inspiration of the Holy Spirit. What is this? Sometimes we feel an intuition, a gentle drawing, a pull, a deep desire, which we sometimes call 'following the flow of love,' or following the flow, or movement, of the Holy Spirit. We follow the inspiration that seems to come from the Holy Spirit working in our spirit.

Let It Flow. Say, "Lord, I cannot heal this person, but I hold myself open to let your Spirit flow through me." Say to him, "I have no power, but let your Spirit flow. Come, Holy Spirit. Heal that person through me, Jesus." See the Spirit of Jesus reaching out and blessing others through you. As we open the door and stand aside, giving the Spirit an opportunity to flow through us, we become coworkers in miracles.

Linda Schweiger of Richland, Washington, tells of being healed of multiple sclerosis, severe depression, and food allergies when a woman was praying over her at a "Life in the Spirit" seminar. She felt power and light go through her body and heard the Lord say, "It is time." Later the Lord showed her that the power and light were his compassion flowing through the compassionate hearts of the woman and the backup pray-ers who joined in praying in the Spirit.

Your Unique Position. You are God's representative and in a unique position to be an instrument of miracles for specific people. I believe the Lord sometimes creates relationships just so that in a time of crisis there will be an openness to receive a miracle, one from the other. The relationship is in place; all you have to do is respond. There may not be anyone else the Lord can call on for that person except you. What if you don't hear him? What if you are too busy to respond?

One time the Lord asked Linda Schubert when she was recovering from a mastectomy to pray for a man in the adjoining hospital room. She resisted at first, and then finally agreed. When she leaned over his bed and whispered that she came to pray, he began to cry, saying, "Today I gave my life to the Lord, and today I was told that I would never see again. You can't know how much your coming in here means to me." Her obedience to the Spirit awakened a spark of life-giving hope in the blind man. Back in her room she made a tearful commitment to respond to the needs of those people God placed in front of her.

Sometimes it's just our presence that the Lord needs. Phyllis C. of South Dakota related a story about being in chapel one day during a Cursillo weekend. "During this time of quiet prayer I was filled with gratitude and praising God for many things. As I was totally swept up in God's love a lady next to me grabbed my arm and said, 'Oh, Phyllis, I've been so unforgiving.' I prayed with her and she left. Although I had said nothing, the presence of the Lord in me seemed to contribute to her arriving at this moment of grace."

Be the Arms of Jesus. If you see a need, pray for that need. Lay hands on the person, intercede, give that healing word. Tell others about the wonders of God. (People love stories.) Bring people into a knowledge of God's Word. St. Augustine said, "Ignorance of Scripture is ignorance of Christ." As we read and study his Word, the Holy Spirit will reveal the character of God, the mercy of God, and the love of God.

Take people to prayer meetings and Bible studies. Invite them to your home for prayer and talk. Draw them into your community and into fellowship. Invite them to gatherings; take them to Mass. Encourage them to be reconciled with themselves, God, church, and family. Be the arms of Jesus that reach out; draw people in close with a hug and say, "I care." Let people know the Jesus in you.

Barbara O. of Escondido, California, tells how her life was transformed after a friend brought her to a Bible study. Sexually abused by her father (whose body was found floating down a river when she was eight), she felt unexplainably guilty and ashamed all of her life. She broke away from the church for thirteen years, had an abortion, and became involved in New Age practices. Drawn back by a friend, she found miraculous transformation through the Word of God. It all began when a friend reached out in love.

The Results Belong to God. Reach out in love and do the best you can. Don't let fear of failure keep you immobilized; the results belong to God. It's your job to ask; it's his job to respond. Pray, turn it over to God in faith, and move on.

KEY POINTS

- Jesus calls us and gives us courage to respond.
- He uses every available person.
- We start with people in our environment.
- As we act on what he says, more will follow.
- His gifts flow as we step out in obedience and follow the promptings of the Holy Spirit.
- Follow the flow of love.
- In Scripture we come to know God.
- We are the arms of Jesus, bringing miracles.
- We pray, and leave the results to God.

PRAYER

Heavenly Father, please forgive us for the times we have ignored the promptings of the Holy Spirit, thus dulling our spiritual sensitivity and preventing miracle blessings for your hurting people. We apologize for the times we have said, "Here I am... send someone else." Please remove from us the effects of those wrongs and give us a new grace of obedience.

Come, Spirit of courage, and lead us beyond our comfort zones, beyond our limitations, into areas where we must depend totally on you. We step out now, as you lead us, with faith in your power to do what is humanly impossible.

Come, Spirit of courage. We will follow the flow of your love and leave the results to you. In Jesus' name we pray. Amen.

EIGHT

Questions and Answers

... the laity, dedicated to Christ and anointed by the Holy Spirit, are marvelously called and wonderfully called and wonderfully prepared so that ever more abundant fruits of the Spirit may be produced in them.

Constitution on the Church[1]

In the miracle survey, almost everyone had questions about miracles. Some are answered in other chapters of this book; others are presented in this section; some may remain unanswered. As you go to the Lord in prayer, trust that he will continue to fill in the gaps for you.

Q: Is it acceptable to ask the Lord for little miracles, such as the healing of colds and finding parking places? Some people say we should not bother God with little things.

A: Everything that builds a relationship with the Lord is important to him. Mary May of Carlsbad, California, shared about her six-year-old daughter falling off a swing set and cutting open her chin. Blood was pouring down her face and she was screaming. When Mary laid hands on her and prayed in tongues, the bleeding immediately stopped and the cut closed. The Lord also took away all of the child's fear.

Asking for help in everyday situations will develop in us a habit of turning to him, which will help in greater trials. Annette Grasso of Portland, Oregon, shared her experience of falling three stories out of a building. As she was tumbling through the air she cried out to the Lord, "Show me how to fall!" He responded, "Fall straight." When she landed, the impact was spread out over her whole body, and not just in one place. Although she was injured, she survived the fall and fully recovered. What struck me about her story was her total trust in a crisis. That kind of trust grows in committed, faithful relationships. Continue to ask about large things and small things. Start establishing that relationship now. Jesus knows what's around the corner in your life, and in the lives of those for whom you pray. "... build yourselves up in your most holy faith...." (Jude 20).

Q: **Does praying in tongues help to release miracles?**

A: We have just scratched the surface in our understanding of the power of the charismatic gift of tongues. As we bypass the natural mind and allow the Spirit to pray through us, the Lord accomplishes more than the mind can begin to comprehend. An illustration that comes to mind involves a woman in northern California whose son was in the hospital, dying of a drug overdose. She cried out to God in tongues to save her boy. Back and forth she marched beside his bed, piercing heaven with her cry. Her son was miraculously healed. We cannot comprehend the miracle power released when we pray in tongues.

When Barbara O. (the sexually abused woman mentioned in Chapter 7, whose friend took her to a Bible study) yielded to the gift of tongues, the power of God was so powerful that she cried and hid her face. She felt the words, "Be not ashamed," being written on her heart. She saw between God and herself a veil of blood, and knew through that vision that God did not see her as she saw herself, but through the veil of the blood of Jesus. The gift of tongues has an enormous value in sensitizing us to the actions of the Holy Spirit. "In the same way, the Spirit helps us in our weakness. We do not know what we ought to pray, but the Spirit himself intercedes for us with groans that words cannot express" (Romans 8:26).

Q: Is everyone called to pray for miracles?

A: I believe so. Miracles are a part of the Lord's indwelling life. Everyone who is surrendered to Jesus shares in the power of the Holy Spirit promised in Scripture, given in confirmation, and released through baptism in the Holy Spirit. It is the Spirit within us, working through us, that effects miracles. When people cry out to him he sometimes sends you and me to help. Sometimes he works directly.

Q: Shouldn't those through whom God works miracles be holy people?

A: Some people believe that the Lord will use only very holy persons, and, therefore, he won't use them because they know their own sinfulness. One of the ways he calls us to holiness, I believe, is through service. The

Decree on the Apostolate of the Laity states: "The Holy Spirit... sanctifies the People of God through the ministry and the sacraments...."[2]. Letting him flow through us with miracles for others can draw us into increasing holiness of life.

Q: How do we break through the barriers of skepticism and a strong intellect which impede the action of the Holy Spirit?

A: A survey respondent, Mary F. from Oceanside, California, expressed her struggle in this area: "I have had miraculous healings; I have witnessed two physical healings; yet skepticism still lingers on. I always wonder—were they really healed?"

We need to guard our minds against the worldview of a weak gospel. We are trained to expect nothing, to avoid getting our hopes up. In my early years in the priesthood in Birmingham, Alabama, I was active in many social and civil rights issues and became so preoccupied with human efforts that I began to question the saving power of the gospel. It was only after I was baptized in the Holy Spirit and began to see God's power that my own deeper conversion began.

Today, in spite of the miracles I have seen around the world, I must confess that I am still being converted. The challenge for each of us is to become as children in our hearts: simple, humble, little, and open. In Scripture Jesus says, "... unless you change and become like little children, you will never enter the kingdom of heaven" (Matthew 18:3). We need to continually surrender our worldliness to allow the Spirit to move.

In that simplicity we learn to proclaim the truth to

our own spirits, to fill our minds with Scripture, spiritual reading, and things of God. As we proclaim God's truth to our minds over and over, we cut a new path in our brain for a new habit to form. We learn to believe; we develop habits of faith. "You were taught, with regard to your former way of life, to put off your old self,... to be made new in the attitude of your minds..." (Ephesians 4:22-23). Unless we are rooted in a faith-filled community, the world will exert an eroding influence on our relationship with Jesus Christ. When Jesus Christ is fully accepted in our hearts, there is no room for the barriers of skepticism.

Q: **If you could name one thing that you think would make a person a candidate for a miracle, what would that be?**

A: Need. At one time there was a ministry in California called the "End of the Rope" Prayer Group. They specialized in impossible situations and often received miracles. When people come to the end of natural solutions and human resources the Lord is free to intervene in amazing ways.

Father Gene Wilson, C.PP.S., of East Palo Alto, California, shared that in the black tradition there is a well-known statement of faith in God's ability to "make a way through no way." When we are at the end of our resources we are more willing to let God do it any way he wants. He is free to take over when we are at the "end of our rope." "He will call upon me and I will answer him; I will be with him in trouble, I will deliver him and honor him" (Psalm 91:15). We find his mercy when we come to the end of ourselves.

Q: **Why are some people healed one day and their problems return the next?**

A: It could be that the external symptoms of the problem are healed but the root problem remains. When this happens the person may need to search out the root problem. There may be a deeper area that needs attention. The Lord wants to go down beneath the symptom and reach the cause. Ongoing, deep forgiveness may be necessary, especially for people with degenerative illnesses.

Also, sometimes there is an emotional experience of healing during healing services that people assume applies to their physical condition when it may not. A surge of healing energy envelops them with a great sense of well-being, and then in a few days it is gone. This does not invalidate the work the Lord accomplished in that experience, even if the person misunderstands what has happened.

Then, again, some people may not fully want to be well. For example, a thirteen-year-old girl in California was born deaf in one ear. At a healing seminar she asked for prayer for the healing of her deaf ear. The community prayed for her, God opened her ear, and she could hear perfectly. In the next few days, however, she found the extra noise so distracting that she didn't want the healing. The deafness returned and has remained.

The Lord works with us where we are, respecting our free will. He offers us gifts of healing to nurture and protect with thanksgiving and faith. Many times in prayer he will ask the question, "What do you really want?" We need to discover our deepest desires, and then allow the Holy Spirit to bring those desires into unity with the Lord's perfect will.

Q: How does a person properly 'receive' a miracle?

A: One way is through thanksgiving. Don't wait for a manifestation; thank God for hearing, for responding, for meeting all your needs, for your very life. Thanksgiving is an action which produces faith, and moves us into an interior position of heart that invites miracles.

Secondly (with prudence and without being foolhardy), reach out and do something that you couldn't do before. Flex the arm, bend, walk, stretch.

Q: When we pray for a person and miracles don't happen, what then?

A: The results belong to God. Trust that he is working even without apparent results. Keep on praying. Ask the Lord to show you how to pray. Perhaps the person seeking a miracle has blockages that can be discovered through a word of knowledge. Again, getting people to the place where they can forgive deeply from the heart often helps in releasing the grace of miracles.

Sometimes the Lord will bring an instantaneous release from one circumstance and leave another. Perhaps one deliverance was necessary in order for the person to take the next step of relationship with him. Perhaps an instantaneous cure of everything would cause us to walk away again. Some do. Jesus healed ten men who had leprosy and only one came back to praise God (Luke 17:15). He wants us to learn a new way of life in him, and sometimes that means keeping us close for a while through a need. Continue to pray, ask, seek, trust, love, and surrender to Jesus as best you can. Ask for the grace to continue praying with expectancy when no change is visible.

Q: What about people who want to stay sick? What about those who don't really want to receive a miracle?

A: First of all, even if you know this is true, do not accuse the person. Jesus has a deep respect for human dignity and free will. Some people have given up trying to be well. Living as a sick person can carry less responsibility than living as a well person. Some people hold onto their illnesses because of the attention they receive from their families. A deep psychological change may be needed in order for a person to begin again to choose life (Deuteronomy 30:19). Some prayer ministers who discern this fact will simply quietly pray for the individual to be able to choose life again.

Q: Do people often receive miracles through the sacraments of the church?

A: Yes! The sacraments all represent the touch of Jesus. They are all visible signs of his presence which help develop relationship with him. Many people have stories of healing and miracles through the sacrament of reconciliation. The Eucharist is most often associated with miracles. Johnny's story in Chapter 14 is a powerful testimony of miracles through the sacraments.

The next time you go to Mass, ask the Lord to reveal one miracle you should seek during Communion. Picture the Lord saying as he hands you the Eucharist, "With my Body, with my Blood, comes the power to work miracles; to go above the power of created nature; to do that which nature cannot do." Picture the Lord giving you the Eucharist for healing and miracles. "Lord, I believe. Say but the word and I shall be healed."

Q: What are some things I can do to increase my faith?

A: As previously mentioned, one important action that produces faith is thankfulness. Ask the Lord to develop in you an appreciation for everything in your life, down to the smallest detail.

Environment is very important. Spend time with people who are seeking the same kind of faith. "... faith comes from hearing the message, and the message is heard through the word of Christ" (Romans 10:17). We hear the message of faith in our environment; we hear it from the Lord in prayer; we read it in Scripture.

Testimony is important. When you tell others what the Spirit has done and is doing in your life, you will be helping others build faith for miracles. As you hear other people's testimonies, your own faith will grow. Write your testimony; print it; give it away, wherever you go. In this way you will be an instrument of multiplied miracles, potentially extending beyond your life-time.

After Phyllis C. of South Dakota was baptized in the Holy Spirit, she read a testimony about a man who was instantly cured of smoking and was inspired to seek such a release for herself. "I had smoked for twenty years," the man explained, "and knew that's what I wanted. When Sister Rosemary Ford, OSB, of Yankton, South Dakota, was praying an inner healing prayer with me, I told the Lord that when she brought up smoking through a word of knowledge, I would be healed of the desire to smoke. That's exactly what happened. I've been totally delivered of cigarettes since 1978."

Use whatever faith you have. The Lord says, "... if you have faith as small as a mustard seed, you can say to this mountain, 'Move from here to there' and it will move. Nothing will be impossible for you" (Matthew 17:20). Do what you can with what you have. Act as if you have faith by stepping out and praying with what little faith you have.

Finally, ask the Lord to increase your faith. The Lord told the father of a demonized boy, "Everything is possible for him who believes." Immediately the boy's father exclaimed, "I do believe; help me overcome my unbelief" (Mark 9:23-24).

Q: Do you think it is important to document and authenticate miracles?

A: Proof is always nice to have and seldom easy to obtain. French theologian Rene Laurentin in *Miracles in El Paso?* reflects on the problem of authenticating miracles and suggests that identifying the most extraordinary aspects is not the most important thing. "What is important is the source of the quality of love involved, since it is God's love that cures and the communication of His love that lifts human means and capabilities above themselves. For such marvels no geometric proof is possible." The test, Fr. Laurentin says, is the one set by Jesus in the words, "Come and see."[3]

Q: Can you describe an environment in which miracles regularly occur?

A: There is a statement in *Miracles in El Paso?* that addresses this question. The author went to El Paso, which is a Texas town on the Rio Grande river near Juarez, Mexico, to study the amazing events occurring around Father Rick Thomas' work with the poor. According to the publisher's note in his book, "What he discovered was a resurgence of God's marvels, the kind that occurs wherever Jesus Christ is completely accepted."[4] In that same environment, Sister Linda Koontz, a member of the National Service Committee with an outreach to the poor in Juarez/El Paso commented about the people's conversion of spirit: "They work better, with heart and joy, and get things done more quickly. They forgive each other. That also is new. Hatred, hard feelings are gone from here. It is simply a conversion to charity and justice. And if physical healing is common, it is because there has first been a healing of the heart, which is more important."[5]

In the following story Betty's mother tenaciously held onto Jesus, believing his word against all odds. Allow the Holy Spirit to bring you to deeper faith through her story.

The Betty Baxter Story. The testimony of Betty Baxter is a perfect illustration of God fulfilling his Word to one who will believe him for it. Betty Baxter was born a twisted cripple. She had knots all over her body. She was fed intraveneously for fourteen years. All those years her mother said, "All things are possible to him that believeth. I believe that Jesus will come and make my daughter normal." She said that for fourteen years. She never wavered from her confession. She watched her crippled, deformed daughter grow without change for fourteen years and she would say, "The Bible says all things are possible to him that believeth." She hung a dress by her daughter's bedside and put a pair of shoes nearby. She would say, "Someday my little girl will wear her dress and shoes to church." But the girl was so deformed nobody ever believed her.

While the mother stood on God's Word, nobody else believed God with her. The husband didn't. The pastor didn't. Her friends didn't. Nobody did.

Every day for fourteen years she reminded Jesus of that scripture. She would say, "I believe for you to come, Jesus, and make my daughter normal." One Sunday afternoon at three o'clock, the wind began to blow around the house and the curtains began to rustle in the breeze, but the sun was out and everything was calm and quiet outside. All of a sudden a white cloud appeared in the living room and it got bigger and bigger. Soon it was real big. Then instantly in the middle of that white cloud Jesus appeared. He stepped out of the white cloud onto the floor and walked over within two steps of the wheelchair and looked at that little crippled girl. She reached out to touch him but she couldn't reach him. The mother said, "Jesus, if you will step a little bit closer she can touch you." He wouldn't move. He stood still. The little girl kept reaching out to touch him but she couldn't. She strained with all her might to touch him but she couldn't. She reached so long, she finally fell onto the floor exhausted. She was a twisted, pitiful heap.

Then Jesus said, "I just wanted you to know that all of your effort without me can get you nothing." Then he took one step closer and touched her. Instantly the knots on her body dissolved. The bones cracked and her limbs straightened. Her body was completely made whole in a moment of time. She jumped up and ran.

Nobody had believed God to heal that little girl except her mother.

That night that little girl, Betty Baxter, stood in her church wearing that new dress and shoes. She had never worn a dress before, nor shoes because her body had been so twisted and deformed. Nobody preached that night. The news spread rapidly and people came from miles around to see God's miracle. Many people got saved, healed, and delivered that night. The power of God was present in a mighty way. Today, Betty Baxter ministers to others. Doctors bring their impossible cases to her and God heals them. Her testimony is, "Nothing is impossible to him that believeth."

KEY POINTS

- Asking builds a relationship with the Lord.
- Praying in tongues helps open us to the gifts of the Spirit.
- As his coworkers we are all called to pray for miracles because they are part of the Lord's indwelling life.
- Allowing the Lord to flow through us with miracles can draw us to increased holiness.
- We can develop new habits of faith to replace skepticism.
- Impossible situations are opportunities for miracles.
- If a root cause is not healed, an illness can return.
- Thanksgiving moves us into a position of heart that invites miracles.
- When miracles don't happen we continue to pray, ask, seek, trust, love, surrender, and leave the results to God.
- Some people need deep psychological change to be able to choose life.
- Many people receive miracles through the sacraments.
- To increase faith it helps to develop an attitude of gratitude, be in an environment of faith, give testimony, use what faith we have, and ask the Lord to increase faith.
- An environment of miracles occurs wherever Jesus Christ is completely accepted.

PRAYER

Come, Holy Spirit. Take every concern, every doubt, every unanswered question. We give them all to you and trust you to sort everything out. Holy Spirit, come and examine our hearts. Reveal those things deep within that block the flow of your grace. Touch and heal, in Jesus' name. Amen.

NINE

Do You Believe?
Survey Responses

... if we really love the Church, the main thing we must do is to foster in it an outpouring of the divine Paraclete, the Holy Spirit....   **Pope Paul VI¹**

Little Blue Flowers. "When I was eight years old I planted some little blue flowers in the back yard of our Oregon home. Every day after school I would rush home to check on my flowers. I watered them and weeded them and fed them special plant food. I really loved my little blue flowers.

"One evening the TV weatherman issued a warning about a killer frost expected that particular night. He said plants would die from the cold. While my parents were talking to each other about the frost, I slipped out the back door and went over to my flowers. The earth was damp and cold beneath the plastic feet of my red flannel sleepers. 'Lord Jesus,' I whispered in the darkness as I gently touched the petals, 'I love my little blue flowers and I don't want them to die. Please protect them from the frost. Amen.' In the frost, which continued for several days, all the plants in our yard were damaged except my little blue flowers. They stood so tall and bright and healthy above the icy sheet of white that my father questioned me in amazement. I explained simply, 'Daddy, I prayed.'

"I've never forgotten what the Lord did for me that evening, so many years ago. It was such a little thing, compared with all the desperate needs in the world; yet it wasn't little to me, and I don't think it was little to the Lord. He revealed his love through the little blue flowers and gained my heart" (Patty Hansen, Beaverton, Oregon).

Summary of Survey Responses. One hundred fifty people responded to our miracle survey, which was given indiscriminately to any charismatic Catholics willing to help. We wanted to understand what people were feeling, thinking, and saying on the subject. We do most of our work on the basis of surveys, so it is reflective of popular sentiments. Their answers are summarized below. How would you have answered the questions?

Do you Believe in Miracles? Each of the respondents answered "Yes" to this question. When asked, "When did you come to believe?" Rhea M. of Bellevue, Washington, answered: "When I was two years old I had polio and was not expected to live. My mother let me know how God wanted me to live, and I did. That's when I first believed!" Peg M. of Puyallup, Washington, answered: "I have believed most of my life, but especially since 1975 when God healed my epilepsy after fourteen years of seizures."

THE GENERAL BREAKDOWN IS AS FOLLOWS:

52—since childhood; many many years; always
35—when personally healed or after witnessing a relative or friend being healed
26—gave a specific date with no details
14—after baptism in the Holy Spirit
 8—through reading the lives of the saints and hearing about Lourdes and Fatima
 6—through reading or hearing Bible stories

2—through reading Christian healing books (Agnes Sanford's *The Healing Light*[2] and Francis MacNutt's *Healing*)[3]
1—after the sacrament of reconciliation
1—after first sacrament of reconciliation as a child
1—after first Communion
1—through Alcoholics Anonymous
3—no answer

DO YOU BELIEVE GOD WANTS TO DO A MIRACLE IN YOUR LIFE?

138—yes
9—unsure
1—no (I already received one)
2—no answer

HAVE YOU EVER BEEN AN INSTRUMENT OF MIRACLES FOR OTHERS?

90—yes
25—no
28—not sure
7—no answer

WOULD YOU LIKE TO BE?

129—yes
0—no
14—no answer
1—don't know (it might be scary)
1—I'm neutral
5—if God wills

WHAT MIRACLE DO YOU DESIRE?

Physical

alcoholism
arthritis
back
cancer
childhood sexual abuse
colon
compulsions
depression
diverticulosis
drug addiction
eyesight
fertility
fibroid uterus
food allergies
healing of diabetes
hemorrhage
hernia
joints
leg pain
Lyme's disease
muscle spasms
rheumatic heart
right arm
ulcerative colitis

Other

anger
anxiety disorder
baptism in Spirit
broken friendship
broken heart
broken marriage
Christian husband
conversion
emotional abuse
employment
faithfulness to Lord
family relationships
fear of failure
memories
prejudice
purification of heart
relationship with God
religious community
spiritual unity
self-image
to be a better witness
to evangelize
to hear God's voice
total surrender
transformation of church
trust in the Lord
unforgiveness

HAVE YOU WITNESSED MIRACLES IN YOUR LIFE OR IN THE LIVES OF OTHERS?

146—yes
2—no
1—slow only
1—no answer

WHAT KINDS OF HEALING HAVE YOU WITNESSED?

Physical 147—Yes
6—No
4—No answer
Psychological 115—Yes
30—No
5—No answer
Spiritual 130—Yes
20—No
6—No answer

DESCRIBE THE MOST DRAMATIC MIRACLE YOU EVER WITNESSED OR HEARD ABOUT FROM FAMILY OR FRIENDS.

(Some of the miracles listed below occurred in large healing services; some at Medjugorje, Yugoslavia; most in ordinary circumstances where people came together to pray.)

arthritis   hearing
atrophied leg   hernia
backs   heart problems

birth defects
blindness
blood poisoning
blood pressure
bone spurs
brain damage
broken rib
bunions
burn victims healed of pain
cancer (many)
cigarette addictions
colds
cripple
degenerative kidney disease
depression
diabetes
diphtheria
dramatic weather change
drug and alcohol addictions
emphysema
endometriosis
eye ulcers
fertility
foot lengthening
headaches

hemorrhage
knees
leg lengthening
lupus
multiple sclerosis
nervous breakdown
person raised from the dead
protection in accident
protection in war
psychological abuse
recurring nightmare
restored breast
restored limbs
shoulder
speech impediments
spinal meningitis
stroke
stuttering
tuberculosis
tumor
weak bladder
withered leg restored

HOW DID KNOWING ABOUT OR EXPERIENCING IT CHANGE YOUR LIFE?

The following are a few representative samples of the total responses.

(All but five people reported a powerful impact from the miracles. The most significant changes were increased faith, commitment, and trust.)

- "When a woman crippled from the waist down got out of her wheelchair and walked after prayer, I was deeply humbled and filled with awe. It gave me greater incentive to continue to pray for the broken Body of Christ and a deeper awareness of the power of intercessory prayer" (Father Pat Crowley, Chino Hills, California).

- "When a lady dying of cancer whom we had prayed for was healed and walked out of the hospital, it gave me courage to share with others that God can work miracles in their lives too" (JoAnn Miller, Mukwonage, Wisconsin).

- "When a person with 'terminal' cancer was healed through prayer it deepened my faith in the Lord's healing love" (Father Ralph Weishaar, O.F.M., San Luis Rey, California).

- "When I was healed of an incurable disease called tic douloureux, which attacks the fifth cranial nerve, I was led into a personal relationship with Jesus, into teaching a Bible study, and into praying for others to be healed" (Angie Lake, Rancho La Costa, California).

- "God became more personal to me after I witnessed the restoration of hearing in a person with a permanently damaged ear bone" (Don Hutter, Arlington, Washington).

- "When Jeff was dramatically healed of a malignant tumor in the chest it made me a real believer in miracles and God's love" (Lenora M., Forest Grove, Oregon).

- "My faith skyrocketed when God dramatically answered my prayer for a weather miracle on a U.S. Coast Guard cutter in Alaska" (Mike Hanratty, Astoria, Oregon).

- "A 62-year-old fallen-away Catholic was totally healed of lung cancer a month before he was expected to die. This answer to prayer increased my faith and boldness to believe God for even greater miracles!" (Kay Sprung, Battle Ground, Washington).

- "When we heard a story about the healing of blindness, it strengthened our faith in the Lord" (Pat and Susan Kirby, Florence, Oregon).
- "A woman recovering from surgery on a shattered leg was walking with a limp. After prayer she no longer limped and had all the pins and screws removed. This made me realize how much the Lord wants us healed and how we must tell others of the love and concern Jesus has for them" (Muriel Neveux, Lawrence, Massachusetts).
- "A friend's leg was lengthened so that he no longer needed an elevated shoe. He is still in awe of what God did for him. It confirmed my belief that God still performs miracles today" (Margaret O., Bend, Oregon).
- "When a prayer group friend was miraculously healed of terminal cancer it deepened my faith in God's desire to heal his people" (Joyce Buzzard, Estacada, Oregon).
- "When I was miraculously healed of epilepsy after fourteen years of seizures it changed my life. I became free, joyous, and filled with purpose in life" (Peg M., Puyallup, Washington).
- "My granddaughter was prayed over and miraculously healed of a heart problem at a prayer meeting in Yankton, South Dakota, in 1987. I have always believed in miracles, but this experience reminded me that all we have to do is have faith and ask. I pray for that faith in my life" (Peggy Stolp, Lincoln, Nebraska).
- "My daughter's miraculous healing deepened my faith; yet my change from loving God to falling in love with him came after my baptism in the Holy Spirit. There is no comparison to the past and now" (Rhea Marchetti, Bellevue, Washington).
- "When I heard about a young girl who was the only survivor of a plane crash, it occurred to me that the

Lord had a purpose for her life. Then I thought maybe he had a purpose for me too. That recognition gave me courage to go on with my life" (O. Mittskus, Carlsbad, California).

Some other answers included: bolder faith; faith strengthened; faith renewed; faith deepened, faith confirmed, faith increased; increased determination to use the faith I have been given; increased faith in the power of prayer; built faith in a living, personal God.

Deeper commitment; greater incentive to pray; deeper desire to serve; deeper hunger for more of God; more open to God; deeper love for the Lord; increased trust (many).

Feeling special; it made his love real; I knew he was alive and real; awe; deeper love for him; God, more personal; more aware of his love and caring.

Easier to let go of petty anxieties; easier to forgive; not as negative; more hopeful; increased gratitude for life; increased sense of purpose.

Need to tell others; courage to speak of his goodness; deep desire to tell others of Jesus' love and concern for them; courage to go on with my life.

The Multiplication of the Lime. In *Miracles in El Paso?* many stories are told of multiplication of food to feed the poor, such as tamales, apples, squash, and grapes. The following story is about multiplication of lime for plastering houses: "We were plastering a warehouse 140 feet long, 32 feet wide and 10 feet high. We had enough sand and cement but only 70 pounds of lime for plastering. We could not buy any because one man had bought it all. The construction foreman and I prayed and in faith went ahead with the plastering. After three days of plastering, the pile of lime had not gone down, even though we had used a lot. We continued to plaster and finished 72 feet of wall with the 70 pounds we had.

Ordinarily, 70 pounds of lime would be enough for only 20 feet of wall. Moreover, the pile did not give out until the day when I was able to buy more lime in a hardware store in town."[4]

Forty-Two Cans of Paint. Pat Mullins, leader of the Ephesians 1:4 Prayer Community in Dublin, California, tells a slightly different story of how God can provide when there isn't enough: "I had a house to paint and a friend with a large supply of surplus paint left over from various jobs. Cash was not a resource for me but my friend's paint was available. He told me to take what I needed.

"Using an available can of white base, I mixed a variety of colors and ended up with five gallons of pleasing color. Knowing that I could never duplicate the color, I tried to make sure there was enough before I started the job.

"I ran out of paint in the middle of the job. Returning to the surplus paint bin I began mixing colors again. This time the only available base color was apricot. I prayed and mixed and prayed and mixed; when I finished I had the exact same color as the previous time. A professional seeing the colors side by side in the house would not be able to tell where one left off and the other began.

"Next, I needed a semi-gloss enamel for trim. Back at the bin I prayed and mixed 18 quarts and portions of six different gallon cans and ended up with the exact same color as the previous two times.

"Sitting in the corner of the garage is a reminder of God's miracle: 42 paint cans. The moral to the story is this: When we are willing to let God be our source and resource (although his methods may seem strange) the results are delightful. The fact is that God could have provided money for paint. His guidance was to use what was at hand."

KEY POINTS

- In the survey most people who believe in miracles arrived at their faith in their early formative years.
- Many came to new or deeper faith in miracles after witnessing or experiencing them personally.
- Often the event had such a great impact that the specific date is imbedded in the mind.
- Generally those who believe in miracles also know God wants to do miracles personally for them, and have been (or would like to be) instruments of miracles.
- Almost all who believe have witnessed miracles.
- God wants to be our source and resource.

PRAYER

Come, Spirit of knowledge, and do your own survey in our hearts. Do we really believe in miracles? Do we believe you want to do miracles in our lives? Have we been instruments of miracles? Would we like to be? What miracles do we need? Have we witnessed miracles? How has witnessing or experiencing miracles changed us? Come, Spirit of knowledge, and show us where we stand with this subject of miracles. Take us forward from that point. Form us, equip us. Come, Spirit of knowledge, and plant your truth deep in our hearts. In Jesus' name we pray. Amen.

TEN

Prayer

Come, Holy Spirit, fill the hearts of Your faithful and kindle in them the fire of Your divine love. When You send forth Your Spirit, they are created; and You renew the face of the earth. **Come, Holy Spirit, Prayer**

The following prayer covers areas of forgiveness common to people everywhere, with special emphasis on father and mother because most of the deepest hurts come from primary relationships. Experience has shown that one of the most significant needs of the healing and miracle ministry is the emptying of oneself from all bitterness, resentment, and unforgiveness that have built up over the years. It also covers thanksgiving, blessing, renewal of baptismal promises, the creed, release of the Holy Spirit, the gifts of the Spirit, and specifically the gift of miracles.

My prayers are united with yours for a mighty release of miracles. Holy Spirit, come in power upon this person right now. Bring deep yielding and great expectation. Enable this person to walk, run, and live in the realm of the miraculous.

Forgiveness. Heavenly Father, I ask today that you help me to forgive everyone in my life. I know that you will give me strength to forgive. I thank you that you love me more than I love myself, and want my happiness more than I desire it for myself.

Lord Jesus, I want to be free from the feelings of resentment, bitterness, and unforgiveness for the times I thought you sent death, hardship, financial difficulties, punishments, and sickness into my family. I let go of all negativity toward you now, especially for all unanswered prayer.

Lord, I forgive myself for my sins, faults, and failings. For all that is truly bad in myself or all that I think is bad, I do forgive myself. I forgive myself for any delving into the occult and calling upon powers apart from you. I forgive myself for times I have ignored the promptings of your Spirit and failed to reach out to those in need. I forgive myself for any unbelief in miracles, and for allowing myself to become contaminated by false doctrines. I forgive myself for all the ways I have broken the covenant with you; for resisting your love; for not praying; and for trying to do things in my own power.

I forgive my mother for all the times she hurt me, resented me, and punished me. I forgive her for the times she told me I was unwanted, or not what she expected. I forgive her for any ways she failed to pray for me; for discouraging me from getting my hopes up; for bruising my childlike faith. For any ways she closed the door to deep faith I do forgive her today.

I forgive my father for any non-support, lack of love, and lack of attention. I forgive him for any ways he failed as a role model; for lack of strength as a Christian leader; for lack of faith; for any ways he made it harder for me to be a coworker in miracles. I forgive him for any ways he distorted the image of God; and for any ways he interfered with my ability to surrender to God. For all that he did that opened the door to unbelief I forgive him today.

Lord, I forgive everyone in my life who made it harder for me to yield and respond to you: sisters and brothers, children, friends, in-laws, relatives, coworkers, and employers. I forgive my teachers for turning me away from you. I especially forgive everyone in my life who trained me in unbelief. I bring to you, Lord Jesus, the one person who did the greatest damage to my relationship with you. I let go of all resentment; I truly forgive. Thank you for setting me free. Come, Holy Spirit, with a miracle of forgiveness today. In Jesus' name. Amen.

Thanksgiving. Heavenly Father, I come before you in praise and thanksgiving for the gift of life. Thank you for sending your Son Jesus; thank you for the free gift of salvation; thank you for the Holy Spirit so generously given to all who ask.

Thank you for my church and all the ways it has drawn me closer to you. Thank you for the sacraments; thank you for the priests, religious brothers and sisters, and lay leaders of the church who have been a part of forming my miracle history.

Thank you for the faith of my ancestors, for the example of my relatives, and your many coworkers who evangelized me over the years. Thank you for family, friends, health, home, work, freedom, and country and civic leaders. Thank you for the many helpful, holy influences you brought to help me along the way. Thank you for my life, exactly the way it is at this present moment. I receive it as a gift from you.

Blessing. Heavenly Father, I ask a blessing upon everyone who made a positive contribution to my miracle journey. Bless those who built my faith, raised my hopes, encouraged, and supported me. Bless those who taught me, corrected me in love, showed me how to pray, and pointed the way to you. Bless the models of courage, faith, and hope. Bless those who reached out in love and didn't give up on me; bless those who set me on your miracle path and provided an environment of miracles. Bless each and every one who revealed Jesus to me. Return a blessing to them a hundred-fold, Father, for the blessings they gave to me. "Give, and it will be given to you. A good measure, pressed down, shaken together and running over, will be poured into your lap. For with the measure you use, it will be measured to you" (Luke 6:38).

RENEWAL OF BAPTISMAL PROMISES

Heavenly Father, I come before you now and renew the promises of sacramental baptism. I reject sin; I repent of all the times I have not walked in the way of your truth or obeyed your will for my life. I ask your forgiveness for the times I have hardened my heart to your voice and not responded to your call.

Jesus, you are Lord of my life. I step down from the center of my life and turn control over to you. I place every area of my life under your dominion.

I now reject Satan and all his works, and all his empty promises. I ask forgiveness for myself, my relatives and ancestors for calling upon powers that set themselves up in opposition to the Lord Jesus Christ. I renounce all false worship and all benefits from magical arts. I renounce every power apart from God and every form of worship that does not offer true honor to Jesus Christ. I specifically renounce _____(identify by name). Heavenly Father, let the cleansing, healing waters of my baptism flow back through the generations and purify my family line from contamination by Satan and sin.

THE APOSTLES' CREED

I believe in God, the Father almighty, Creator of heaven and earth. I believe in Jesus Christ, his only Son, our Lord. He was conceived by the power of the Holy Spirit and born of the Virgin Mary. He suffered under Pontius Pilate, was crucified, died, and was buried. He descended to the dead. On the third day he rose again. He ascended into heaven, and is seated at the right hand of the Father. He will come again to judge the living and the dead. I believe in the Holy Spirit, the holy Catholic Church, the communion of saints, the forgiveness of sins, the resurrection of the body, and life everlasting. Amen.

Release of the Holy Spirit. Heavenly Father, I ask you now in the name of Jesus for a fresh outpouring of your Holy Spirit. Baptize me with the fire of your love; fill me to overflowing with your Spirit. Holy Spirit, come; flow into the deepest parts of my life. Holy Spirit, come in power. Holy Spirit, come in compassion. Holy Spirit, come in mercy, purity, holiness, and love. Let the mighty flow of your power so saturate my being that I will be swimming in a river of miracles.

Release of the Nine Charismatic Manifestation Gifts. Heavenly Father, all of the gifts are miracles; and I want them all. Pour out your gift of tongues, interpretation, wisdom, knowledge, discernment, faith, prophecy, healing, and miracles. Thank you, Father! In Jesus' name I pray. Amen.

Release of the Gift of Miracles. Heavenly Father, release in me a special anointing for this gift of dramatic, instantaneous answers to prayer. I pray for a tremendous openness to your gift of miracles. When your Spirit moves me, I want to lay hands on cancer patients and see them healed instantly. When your Spirit moves me, I want to lay hands on broken bones and see them healed in front of my eyes. When your Spirit moves me, I want to lay hands on heart patients and see them instantly cured. When your Spirit moves me, I want to lay hands on people with schizophrenia and see their minds instantly restored. When your Spirit moves me, I want to lay hands on cold, arrogant, indifferent, atheistic persons and see them instantly converted to Jesus Christ. When your Spirit moves me, I want to see signs and wonders everywhere.

I make a commitment to you, Father, to give you all the glory. All power is yours; all glory is yours; all honor belongs to you. I kneel before you as your servant and humbly ask you to use me as an instrument for healing my brothers and sisters and restoring faith in our miracle church.

I now hold myself open to receive manifestations of these gifts under the direction of the Holy Spirit. I accept them with gratitude and joy. Thank you, Father. Thank you, Jesus. Thank you, Holy Spirit. Amen.

PRAYER

Heavenly Father, I bring to you now one person (_____) who needs a miracle. Look upon this person's need and come in miracle power to meet that need. Thank you, Father, in Jesus' name. Amen.

PART III

TO GOD BE THE GLORY

Now to the King eternal, immortal, invisible, the only God, be honor and glory for ever and ever. Amen. **1 Timothy 1:17**

ELEVEN

His Word Is Life
The Miracle Power of Scripture

For the word of God is living and active....
Hebrews 4:12

As you reflect upon the stories in this chapter, ask the Lord
to bring you into a new level of faith in his Word. Have there
been critical moments in your life when a Scripture passage
has had a life-giving significance?

Deadly Poison. "One of many occasions in which God's
protective power was manifest occurred in the course of my
priestly vocation as a retreat master, when I was at a retreat
house in Arizona. Between talks I hurriedly dashed into the
dining room for a quick cup of coffee. I put some instant coffee in a cup and filled it from a large urn labeled 'hot water.'
Gulping it down, I suddenly felt a severe burning pain in my
throat. Staggering into the kitchen, I asked the cook what
was in the urn. She showed me a container marked 'Deadly
Poison—Fatal If Swallowed.' She had been soaking the inside of the urn with this poisonous, caustic chemical to remove the scum and stains.

"Someone called the poison control center; the medic on
duty asked for the ingredients listed on the container, and
then urgently instructed the caller to rush me to the nearest

hospital where arrangements were made for a poison control specialist to meet me. We were too far out in a rural area to request an ambulance. They said if I got there before it was too late, I might live, but they expected permanent throat and voice damage.

"While I was waiting for the car to pick me up for the trip to the emergency room, the Lord spoke to me interiorly, saying, 'Turn to my Word. There is healing power in my Word.' I responded silently, 'Lord, I've never done this before, but when one faces the possibility of dying, it is easy to elicit greater faith. I claim, in faith, your words of Mark 16:17-18: '...signs will accompany those who believe:... when they drink deadly poison, it will not hurt them at all.' Within less than a minute the pain stopped, and I felt perfectly normal. They were still waiting for me in the emergency room!

"It was then that I remembered the words of the psalmist, 'In your distress you called, and I rescued you'" (Father John H. Hampsch, C.M.F., Los Angeles, California).[1]

The Breath of Life. "I had thrombo-phlebitis in my legs. The recommended treatment was hospitalization and the use of a blood thinner. I was admitted to Martin Luther Hospital in southern California.

"One night during my stay in the hospital I woke up out of a sound sleep. I couldn't breathe, and felt like there was a heavy rock on my chest. I tried to take a breath but nothing happened; no air would go into my lungs. I was filled with fear. In the dark room I buzzed the nurse.

"As she entered the room and turned on the light my eyes were drawn to the picture of Jesus on the opposite wall. The instant my eyes lit on the picture I felt his presence. I knew I was dying, but all fear was gone.

"The nurse signalled code blue and everyone came running. When the charge nurse exchanged glances with the nurse at my bedside, she just shook her head. Then the charge nurse (who was not a Christian) recognized me. We had known each other for some time, and were friends. She ran over and scooped me up in her arms. As she did this my whole left side went numb. When I saw the tears streaming down her face, I deeply needed to respond to them, but I couldn't breathe.

"And yet somehow the words came out: 'The Lord is my Shepherd; there is nothing I shall want' (Psalm 23). As I spoke the word of God, air entered into my lungs. They call it the Living Word. The Word of God is the breath of life to me" (Shirley Filadelphia, San Juan Capistrano, California).

Transformed By a Renewed Mind. "In 1978 I was very ill and hospitalized for tests to determine the source of the problem. The visual field in my eyes was poor; my motor coordination was deteriorating; I had lost the ability to write, add, subtract, and divide. A brain scan indicated that at age thirty-three I had the brain of a 95-year-old woman. My skull was collapsing in upon itself so that the surface was bumpy to touch.

"Medical science tells us that brain cells don't regenerate, yet mine did. My miracle was progressive, however. As my relationship with Jesus began to develop I learned to walk in obedience to the Holy Spirit. The Lord gave me three life-changing Scripture verses that I have studied and prayed over for years:

> Yet to all who received him, to those who believed in his name, he gave the right to become children of God.
> **John 1:12**

> For you have been born again, not of perishable seed, but of imperishable, through the living and enduring word of God. **1 Peter 1:23**

> And if the Spirit of him who raised Jesus from the dead is living in you, he who raised Christ from the dead will also give life to your mortal bodies through his Spirit, who lives in you. **Romans 8:11**

"As I held on and pressed in, allowing the Holy Spirit to plant those words deeply in my soul, what he revealed to me was that when I was born of God, even my genetic structure was brought back to its original purity. It didn't matter if it was physical or mental. Because God was my source of life, those things that were destroyed would be brought back to wholeness in spirit, soul, and body.

"Over several years my condition gradually reversed, to the present day when I experience the wholeness he promises in his Word" (Shelah Bliss, Walnut Creek, California).

PRAYER

Heavenly Father, we thank you for your living Word that brought Father Hampsch, Shirley, and Shelah back from the brink of death. Holy Spirit, plant the reality of miracles deep in the hearts of the readers. Let them know that you desire to do even greater things for them, and that your Word will open the door to miracles. In Jesus' name. Amen.

TWELVE

"I'm Not Afraid of the Morning Anymore"
Mary Ann's Story

*Because of the Lord's great love we are not consumed,
for his compassions never fail. They are new every
morning; great is your faithfulness.* **Lamentations 3:22-23**

Before I begin with my testimony I must say that all
through my anguish my mother prayed and prayed and
prayed for a miracle. If she were living today she would be
proud that her grown daughter is not afraid of the morning
anymore.

I was born in Managua, Nicaragua and raised in Costa
Rica, where from infancy people live a very social life. My
mental illness did not become apparent until my preteens.
At that time it became obvious that I preferred the comfort
and security of my room to the birthday parties, swimming,
music, and movies sought after by girls my age.

When my parents were divorced I was devastated. If there
was any feeling of life in me, it was almost completely destroyed at that time. Mother was my life. People used to say I
was much too attached to her. After their divorce I felt dead
inside. Not long after the divorce Mother suffered a massive
stroke, which left one side paralyzed. Emotionally, I too be-

came paralyzed. She eventually recovered, a miracle in itself. I became progressively worse.

Going to school meant leaving Mother and the haven of my room, which terrified me. My two brothers, my sister, and I were sent to boarding school because Mother was unable to care for us. The boys moved to the United States, and my sister and I went to Nicaragua. In the Managua airport enroute to school, Mother turned us over to our aunt and walked away. When my hand was forced out of Mother's, I screamed with horror and became vocally paralyzed. From that moment on I hated my mother, I hated God, the church, and everything else. I hated life.

The first year of school I could hardly talk. Blindly, half alive, I just went through the motions. I would walk to class with my hands covering my face and keep my face covered in class. The only nun I would respond to in class was the one who allowed me to keep my face covered. I used to hope that they would put me in a small locker and let me press buttons to give answers to the teacher.

I hated the sunrise; it meant I would have to pretend I was alive for another day. When summer came and I was home with Mother, I would withdraw even more. I hated Mother; I hated her for getting sick, for separating me from my brothers, for my own emptiness.

Upon the advice of the nuns who reported my increasingly antisocial behavior, mother took me to the Oschner Clinic in New Orleans for psychiatric evaluation. At that time, at age fifteen, I began a seventeen-year odyssey of intensive psychiatric care. I was in and out of every mental hospital in the region (except a state charity hospital), and given every type of treatment possible, except electric shock. Mother refused to permit that particular therapy. I was diagnosed as an incurable, suicidal, chronic depressive. According to the doctors, I would be that way for the rest of my life.

Carefully hoarding my sleeping medicine, antidepressants, and tranquilizers, I planned a fourth suicide attempt. I was determined to take my life. In that fourth attempt I was found unconscious and rushed to the hospital. My body was blue and my mouth was foaming as a priest gave me the last rites. The doctor in charge asked my father, "What did you do to her? She doesn't want to live; we are losing her." Even though on the fourth day I began to respond, the doctor told my family that I would probably be a vegetable the rest of my life.

As my normal body functions returned I looked out at the world with bitter, sad, empty eyes. Four psychiatrists re-di-agnosed me as a classic suicidal manic-depressive; they pre-scribed high doses of lithium along with other medicines.

As I was beginning to respond to the treatment, my brother Bobby, with whom I was very close, was killed in Vietnam. Again my life was blown into pieces. The pain was so great I couldn't even cry. I was beyond pain, for myself and for my family. It wasn't fair. I wanted to die and he didn't. Why didn't God take me instead of Bobby?

After another long interim in the hospital I began to re-spond again. I was able to work, oddly enough, for doctors (who didn't know my psychiatric history), and even excelled in my position.

My biggest breakdown came following the breakup of a romance with a Jewish man. This time I pleaded with Mother to keep me at home without calling the doctor. She gave in when I promised to take my medicine, and for a short while I appeared to my family to be doing okay.

They didn't know about my terrible hallucinations, often with snakes and other horrible things. Mother had a large, beautiful balcony filled with all kinds of plants which I tended for a period of time. One evening I saw horrible-look-ing worms and snails all over the plants and on the ground and all over me. I could even hear them buzzing. I started screaming hysterically, paralyzed with fear. Mother half-car-ried me inside, holding me until I calmed down and reassuring me that there was nothing on the plants or on me.

I had (and still have) a fetish for nightgowns. One night when I was hallucinating I grabbed all my nightgowns and cut them into pieces; laughing and crying hysterically I threw the pieces all over the room. Mother ran into my room and tried to stop me. After hours of struggling I eventually took some medication and calmed down. The following morning my doctor called and asked to see me. Not remembering the events of the previous night, I obediently went to his office. I was immediately admitted to the hospital and placed in restraints. Later I found out that both my mother and father had called the doctor. This was another long- term stay.

After my discharge, Mother, advised by my doctor, went to Nicaragua to tend our coffee farm. Depressed and furious with her for leaving, I slept twenty-four hours a day, getting up only to shower and eat. No one ever seemed to understand that I just didn't want to live.

While she was in Nicaragua, Mother died of a stroke. I was twenty-five years old and unable to handle another stress in my life. Heading for my father's vacant condominium in Slidell, Louisiana, I became an angry recluse. Sleeping all the time, I kept the drapes closed and disconnected the phone. When my father came to check on me one day he found me hiding in a closet.

Again I returned to the hospital. During that period I befriended a boy who was in the hospital because of drug addiction. Something about his deep pain got through to me; I wanted to help him. After my discharge, I was flipping through the television channels one day and saw Danny Abramowitz (an ex-New Orleans football player) on a nun's program. I later discovered it was Mother Angelica's program, Mother Angelica Live, which is carried on the Eternal Word Television Network located in Birmingham, Alabama. When Danny spoke of working with alcohol and drug abusers I thought of my friend in the hospital.

I somehow found the Center for Jesus the Lord on Rampart Street in New Orleans. Sister Olga Rushing, the registrar and person in charge of directing and instructing the inner healing and counseling ministry, answered the phone. I explained that I was seeking Danny to help a friend on cocaine. She replied that Danny was not there. Hearing my personal despair, she invited me to attend a service at the center the following day.

When I opened the door to the center I thought it was the wrong door. How wrong I was. For the first time I had opened the *right door!* The usher took me to the front pew. I later learned that it was a priest retreat and a healing service. Sitting there in wonderment I noticed a priest staring at me. It made me feel uncomfortable. I was sitting down outwardly but inwardly I wanted to curl up in the fetal position.

After the service I met Sister Olga, who took me to Father Emile Lafranz, founder and director of the Center and member of the National Service Committee. Shortly after being with him, he heard my confession and reassured me that Jesus loved me. I looked at him in disbelief and said, "Jesus loves me?" "Yes," he repeated, and encouraged me to return to the center the following Sunday.

During Mass the following Sunday I noticed the priest who had previously gazed at me so intensely. After the final blessing I ran into the sacristy to see him, not knowing who he was. I learned that he was Father Robert DeGrandis.

I was amazed at how much he seemed to intuitively know about me. At his request I agreed to go to a "Life in the Spirit" seminar, without knowing its purpose. Nothing much seemed to happen at the seminar; I didn't feel any different. Yet I knew inside that something had changed.

The next time I saw Father DeGrandis he invited me to a healing service. As Father was praying over a lady during the service, I suddenly realized he was not visible anymore. I had been lifted into a heavenly realm. I heard beautiful music; I saw a big white cloud, and an angel. I was so overwhelmed with joy and love and song that something came bubbling up from deep inside. I was praying in the Spirit. When I left the service Father DeGrandis handed me a copy of the `Forgiveness Prayer'[1] and told me to say it for thirty days.

I began to feel better and better. While all of these spiritual things were going on I cancelled appointments with my doctor. He had strongly advised me to stay away from church. In addition, a priest I had spoken to earlier in connection with my friend on cocaine, advised me to stay away from the charismatic renewal. He said the emotional nature of the renewal could be detrimental to my stability. I didn't listen to either of them.

Because I had cancelled several appointments, the doctor called my father and told him I was beginning to withdraw again. In the past my withdrawal preceded hospitalization. My father ordered me back to therapy, unwilling to believe my new inner strength. I told the doctor I was going through inner healing and attending church and that I was all right.

After six months of inner healing I went to my doctor again and said, "You must listen to me for a change." I told him about inner healing; I told him that I hadn't cried for months; I told him that I wanted to live; I told him that I was not afraid of the morning anymore. He refused to take me off medication, convinced that this was another manic stage.

Father DeGrandis sent me to Elizabeth Sheldon of New Orleans, an associate of his, for deeper inner healing. I went to prayer meetings, praise rallies, conferences, and daily Mass. My whole life had changed. After I heard Father DeGrandis' teaching on the Eucharist, I turned to Mass regularly as a source of ongoing healing. I became more and more alive. I was in love with Jesus, in love with the Center of Jesus the Lord, with people, with the whole world. I was high all right, but not manic.

After a year my doctor took me off several medications and told me to report back periodically. He said he didn't understand what I was doing, and didn't really believe in it, but had to admit that I was different. "Continue what you're doing," he smiled. "I see life in you." As I floated out of his office I said "I feel like the bride of Jesus." He smiled and responded, "I'll be here if you need me." That was in 1986.

I became actively involved with volunteer work in the community, at the Center, and for Father DeGrandis. My family was amazed, hesitant, and pleased. They finally began to believe me following a near-fatal automobile accident in which I severely injured my back and legs. Secure and safe in Jesus during the recovery period, I did not suffer mental regression.

Upon reflection, my turning point seemed to come in the pit of my own despair when I reached out to help someone else. The Lord says, "… if you spend yourselves in behalf of the hungry and satisfy the needs of the oppressed, then your light will rise in the darkness, and your night will become like the noonday" (Isaiah 58:10).

Mary Ann's Prayer.

I pray now for all those who are oppressed and in the darkness of despair and depression. Lord Jesus, I lift them all up to you and ask you to pour out your Holy Spirit through your merciful heart. Send an angel of mercy to minister to them as you ministered to me. Let them know there is life after depression; that there can be an end to depression. Sweet Jesus, just as you opened the door for me, open the door for my brothers and sisters, that they can see and believe that all things are possible through your divine mercy and love.

Lord, I praise you and thank you for healing me and bringing me up from the depths of despair and emptiness; for keeping me safe in you; for making me a new creation. As you so gently and tenderly touched me, touch all of them. I place each of them in your sa-

cred heart and cover them with your precious blood. Lord, have mercy on all in mental hospitals and under psychiatric care. Lord, have mercy; Lord, have mercy; Lord, have mercy.

You are love; you are healing; you are alive in the Eucharist, the miracle medicine for broken and destroyed persons. Lord, I bow before you and thank you for blessing each of these people now. In Jesus' name I pray. Amen.

THIRTEEN

A Promise Fulfilled
Maria Josephine's Story

... God had power to do what he had promised.
Romans 4:21

"When my third child was seven years old," says Tony Montante of Monterey, California, "the Lord spoke to me during a prayer meeting and said, 'Tony, you and Cathy shall have another child, and you will name the child Joseph. Study the meaning of the name.' The Lord's voice was powerful and strong. It seemed to be external, as compared with the inner voice of God that we usually come to know. I said to myself, 'This can't be for me. We don't want any more children.' When I told the prayer group leader he said, 'I think this is for my wife and me. We've never had a child. We will claim the word.'

Months passed. One day the Lord said to me, "Tony, today when I show you a woman I want you to lay hands on her and bless her." I was driving down the freeway at the time, and happened to pass my cousin. I said to myself, "It must be her." The Lord said, "No, it's not her." When I reached home and met my wife at the door, the Lord said it was her. So I laid hands on Cathy and prayed for a blessing, not remembering the earlier prophecy.

Some more months passed. Then one day my wife said, "I'm pregnant." When I responded, "Praise God!" she looked at me and asked, "Are you crazy? We didn't plan on this!" Then I told her about the word I had received in the prayer meeting so many months previously.

Her pregnancy unfolded with great difficulty; high blood pressure added to the many complications. One evening at a prayer meeting, during her pregnancy, my wife received the word: "Blessed is thy fruit. Even though the doctor tells you the child is dead, my word will come true." The word was forgotten until much later.

The obstetrician in Monterey arranged for her to be admitted to Stanford Hospital in Palo Alto, California, when she was six months and three weeks into her pregnancy. Things looked pretty grim.

On the evening of the first day at Stanford, December 30, I decided to bring in a fancy dinner for two from a restaurant. As I returned with our extravagant meal, I saw people running in and out of her room. At her door I listened to shocking news: "We've lost the baby's heartbeat." I said, "That's impossible." They said, "Please leave." I stayed and watched the monitor. Finally the heartbeat came again. I watched it go from 115 to 39 and then disappear again. Again it returned. They decided to give my wife oxygen. Every time she received oxygen the baby's heartbeat increased. I commented on this fact to the doctor. He said it was clinically impossible for the baby to react to the oxygen. I called the nurse and said, "Every time you give my wife oxygen the baby's heartbeat increases. When you remove it the heartbeat decreases. The doctor doesn't believe me." She said nothing. I stayed and continued praying.

In the morning after a consultation, the doctor told me they would give my wife an injection to help the baby's lungs develop. The drug required forty-eight hours to activate.

I felt like Abraham as I walked the halls. God had given

him a promise that made no sense. In his promise to me, all I saw left and right was doom and death. Finally, even though my heart was not ready for it, I came to a place where I was able to commit my wife and baby to God and accept what came, even if they both died.

As I continued to walk the halls the Lord said, "Look at the doorway to your wife's room." I looked up and saw the number seven. Seven stands for perfection. Something broke loose and I began to praise God. As I praised I became stronger. I would keep holding onto God's promise, in spite of the medical verdict. My commitment was one of increasing trust.

At 10:00 a.m. on the day after Cathy's arrival they gave her the injection. Something went wrong, and less than a half-hour later they rushed her to surgery. I was allowed in the room with her during the surgery. She was given a spinal at her request, so that she would be conscious during the procedure.

When I discovered we had a girl, I thought I had blown it. "Lord, you gave me the name Joseph." He responded quietly, "Didn't I tell you to look for the meaning in the name?" The name Joseph means "He shall add on, or increase."

When Maria Josephine was born she weighed one pound and 12 ounces; then she lost three ounces. Everything was wrong with her. She had an enlarged liver, an enlarged heart, an infection in the intestines, a virus, pneumonia, a heart murmur, and two hernias. In the natural plain, she didn't stand a chance.

I kept on praying, concerned about my wife's continuing high blood pressure and my baby's slim hopes. One day God came along again and gave me a vision. In the vision I was walking and crying. When I felt someone reach out and take my hand, I turned and saw my daughter, the new baby, as a teenager. In the vision she said, "Don't worry, Daddy. Everything is fine." The Lord had given me a picture of the future. He was showing me that she would make it.

At 1:00 a.m. on the third day after Maria Josephine's birth, the doctor came to Cathy's room and announced that the baby was not expected to live through the night. When he suggested that we go and see her one last time, my wife said tartly, "You know what, doctor? I want you to please leave my room. Turn out the light and do not come back until morning. When you come back, come back with good news. I am now going to sleep. Good night!" With that she turned over and went to sleep.

The following morning the head pediatrician came into Cathy's room, pulled up a chair and sat down. "Your baby is stable," he said. "Everything is okay. Her heart is okay. All is well. She has no other symptoms to be concerned about. I will give her antibiotics to be on the safe side, but everything is normal."

Sometime during the night and early morning, between 1:00 a.m. and 8:00 a.m., the Lord had miraculously healed Maria Josephine of all the many things wrong with her body: the enlarged liver, the enlarged heart, the infection in the intestines, the virus, the pneumonia, the heart murmur; everything but the hernias. When that surgery was eventually performed, after several delays, the scar totally disappeared in twenty-four hours. She became known at Stanford as the miracle baby.

We had to leave her at Stanford Hospital another two months because she was too small to take home. She was on tubes for only another three days, however, and didn't need a respirator. When she came home she weighed four pounds.

Finally, the medical bill. The charges were $100,000. Our insurance covered 80 percent or $80,000. That left a remaining bill of $20,000. My salary as a tile setter at the Monterey Bay Aquarium would nowhere near provide that kind of cash reserve. Within a short time the Lord raised up a benefactor who covered the full amount.

Reflecting back on these events, I find that it is easier now to expect more and more miracles. The Lord gave a promise and he fulfilled the promise. He has given other promises and has been faithfully fulfilling them also. What I understand is this: He moves regardless of how good or holy we are, or even how obedient we are. He seems to say, "I make this promise, not because you deserve it, but this is how I desire to work in this area." He is sovereign.

TONY AND CATHY'S PRAYER

Heavenly Father, we lift up to you now those people who have had a promise from you and no apparent fulfillment. Give them the faith of Abraham. Give them the grace to hold on, and continue to trust in you, no matter what the circumstances. When they feel their lives are competing with Job, hold them close. Heavenly Father, in your perfect timing, bring your promises to fulfillment. Thank you, Father. In Jesus' name. Amen.

FOURTEEN

"I [Am] No Longer in Control"
Miracles through the Sacraments

He remembers his covenant forever....
Psalm 105:8

Father Richard Woldum of Los Angeles tells this miracle story: One year after my ordination I became a hospital chaplain in Illinois. During my assignment at that location the Lord began to heal some patients. At that time I was not in the charismatic renewal and knew nothing about the gift of healing, but was soon to learn of its reality through the power of the sacraments.

One morning I received a call to come to the emergency room to see an eleven-year-old boy named Johnny, who was dying. I found him on a breathing machine, his head the size of a tire.

Johnny's parents told me that he had been riding his bike on a gravel road near his home when a truck came flying over the hill and hit him head-on. The collision caused him to be thrown into the nearby field. When the ambulance arrived, the medics found his head cut wide open with half his brains scattered in the field. They literally picked up pieces of his brain, shoved them into his head, and took him to the hospital.

When I asked Johnny's parents if he had been baptized, they said, "No." They informed me they attended no church but prayed at home as a family. I asked them if they would like me to baptize Johnny. They glanced at each other as if to say, "It couldn't cause any harm," then said to me, "Go ahead." They also said if I wanted to, I could baptize him into the Catholic faith. That night, with the parents and two nurses as witnesses, I baptized Johnny.

The next morning I was doing communion rounds when my beeper went off. Johnny's doctor wanted me in the intensive care unit. "What you do last night?" he asked in broken English, as I met him outside Johnny's room. I explained to the doctor, a Buddhist, that I had baptized Johnny (with the permission of his parents) so that he could go to heaven. When I asked him why he was so concerned, he informed me that the boy's swelling had disappeared. The doctor was still convinced that the boy would die, however; or if he lived, remain a vegetable, never moving, talking, or even moving his eyes.

That night Johnny's parents thanked me for baptizing him. I then explained about the anointing of the sick, and asked if they would like Johnny to receive that sacrament. With their agreement and in their presence, I anointed Johnny.

The next morning during communion rounds the doctor again paged me on my beeper. He met me at the door of intensive care and directed me to Johnny's room, explaining on the way that he had heard from the nurses that I had again prayed for Johnny.

Then he pointed to Johnny's eyes and asked, "What you do?" I saw that Johnny's eyes were moving. "It was just the power of Jesus through prayers for the sick," I responded. He gave a faintly sarcastic grin and said, "It no matter. Boy no talk or move. He remain vegetable."

It was now the third night, counting the night of the accident. I suggested to the parents that they permit me to give Johnny the sacrament of confirmation. They agreed.

The following morning his legs and arms were moving. The doctor said to me in front of the parents, "I no longer in control." He was simply unable to explain what was happening. The parents turned to me and said they wanted to become Catholics. I recommended that they wait and see what happened to Johnny before making a final decision.

That evening when I explained to them about the Eucharist, they said they wanted this for Johnny, too. I gave him some of the Precious Blood through an eye dropper. The next morning he was making sounds.

The weekend was now upon me. It was Labor Day, 1979, and I went home to celebrate my grandmother's ninetieth birthday. When I checked in on Johnny upon my return, I learned he had been transferred to the third floor, which was the surgery unit. I went upstairs to see him, fearing that he had gone back into surgery. He was sitting on his bed, talking to his mother.

After his recovery they took another x-ray of his head and found that the part of his brain which had spilled out into the field had grown back.

When I eventually talked to Johnny's parents about becoming Catholics, they informed me they would continue praying at home. The doctor in the case started looking into Christianity. Three nurses converted to Catholicism.

FATHER RICHARD'S PRAYER
Heavenly Father, I pray for the readers to receive a supernatural gift of faith in the sacraments of the church. Let the power of baptism come alive to them. Let there be an explosion of faith in the power of sacramental anointing, confirmation, the Eucharist, and reconciliation. Pour out into the hearts of the reader a deep knowledge of the power of the sacraments of holy orders and marriage. Thank you, heavenly Father, in Jesus' name. Amen.

FIFTEEN

Miracles in Medjugorje?
Mary's Intercession for Us

Many, O Lord my God, are the wonders you have done. The things you planned for us no one can recount to you; were I to speak and tell of them, they would be too many to declare. **Psalm 40:5**

The Yugoslavian bishops responsible for discerning the truth of the reported apparitions of the Blessed Mother at Medjugorje have not yet ruled officially. The Catholic church teaches that Catholics are free to decide for themselves whether they accept such apparitions, and any reports of miracles related to them. The following stories are of people who felt their lives touched by God at Medjugorje.

Judy's Miracle. In 1986, Judy Durrant of Calgary, Canada, received the news that she had chronic myelogenic leukemia, a disease for which there is no cure. Her white blood count was 100,000 (normal is 10,000). While the disease was in the early stage, she was given from three weeks to three years to live. The most hope the doctors could give her was a life on chemotherapy with the hope that the blood count would level off.

One month later, Judy heard an inner voice saying, "Don't worry; you will be better." From childhood her faith in God had been strong, and she believed that one day God would heal her. Because of her need for much rest, her parents provided a nanny to take care of her four small children. This gave Judy the opportunity to attend daily Mass and spend more time in prayer seeking the Lord's guidance.

One day after Mass someone introduced Judy to the story of Medjugorje by giving her a video from someone who had been to that mountain village in Yugoslavia. That person anointed Judy with oil blessed in Medjugorje. This blessing brought Judy a tremendous sense of peace. Judy knew she had to go there herself, and arranged with her schoolteacher-husband to make the trip during his three-week December break.

Her doctor objected as her platelets had now risen to two million (normal count is 400,000), and he feared that airplane travel could result in her having a stroke. Judy felt such an urgency, however, that the doctor relented, saying, "Go for it. Maybe she [Mary] can do more for you than I can."

Then Judy received another message: "Go in November." Judy and her husband Dave were in Medjugorje during Thanksgiving week, 1986.

In Medjugorje they joined an English-speaking group. Through the priest on that group Judy received a new appreciation of Mary's role as a model of humility; she reaffirmed her childhood devotion to Mary. Members of the group experienced many healings, both inner and outer. Judy's husband was the first to realize she had been healed because of the unusual energy she possessed as she easily climbed Mt. Krizevac in the bitter cold.

Judy's first blood test after her return home showed her counts on the high side of normal. She stayed on her medication for two more weeks. Her doctor had her return for blood tests every few months.

In 1987, when her parents went to Medjugorje to give thanks for their daughter's good health, they spoke with an Italian doctor who was spending six months in Medjugorje, and with Father Slavko Barbaric, O.F.M., spiritual director of the visionaries at Medjugorje. The doctor and the priest asked Judy's parents to send over medical documentation. Those reports were sent to Medjugorje in April, 1987.

Since that time Judy has traveled around Canada giving testimony of her miraculous healing. In one correspondence with the publisher of the *Medjugorje Star* she wrote: "I give thanks to our Lord and our heavenly Mother every day. God is truly all-loving. It is wonderful to be healthy so that I may care for our four beautiful children. And, of course, tell others of my miracle."

Cindy's Miracle. Cindy was born prematurely and with severe brain damage due to an accident three weeks before she was due. Doctors expected her to die because sucking, swallowing, bowel movements, vision, body movement, and everything involving normal behavior patterns was erased from her brain. She had to be tube-fed and seemed doomed to be institutionalized. With four other small children, her mother couldn't manage the full-time care involved.

Cindy's grandmother, Rose Fabre of New Orleans, then stepped in: "As Cindy's grandmother, I went to the hospital to see what I could do. Three feedings later, Cindy was introduced to the very first discipline of her young life. Through tears of frustration, anger, and determination, I sternly told her, 'Either suck your bottle, Cindy, or Maw Maw isn't going to feed you.' All the time I constantly beseeched Mother Mary to intercede on our behalf. 'Please God, show me the way to reach this child,' was my constant plea. Cindy had to show some sign of response, or we would lose her.

"God heard my cries of anguish. Cindy took her first feeding by mouth that morning. After her fourth feeding by mouth the doctor released her to me.

"Everyone rallied around our little miracle baby. The entire family started a program of prayers and taking turns with Cindy. Days and nights were so intense as to be almost indistinguishable. Colic plagued her every hour. Formulas were changed and everything known to mothers was tried in an effort to keep her comfortable. Doctors told us that Cindy would not grow at a normal rate or develop teeth or good bone structure. Cindy did grow, though teething and colds brought on seizures.

"We took her to Medjugorje, hoping for the miracle. During the first Mass we attended in St. James Church, Cindy's eyes focused on the altar during the offertory. She seemed transfixed and glowing as she listened to the bells. When everyone began to sing the Ave Maria, Cindy joined with "*Aabaee, Aabaee.*" Tears of happiness flowed down my face; these were her first recognizable words.

"She is continuing to make progress. When she is strong enough she will belong with her brothers and sisters."

PRAYER FOR THE INTERCESSION
OF THE BLESSED MOTHER

Heavenly Father, thank you for sending the Blessed Mother to intercede for Judy and Cindy and the countless others who have cried to her in desperate need. Father, please give to the many people praying for miracles an openness to the ministry of the Blessed Mother. Please assign her to intercede for those in desperate need. Thank you, Father. In Jesus' name. Amen.

SIXTEEN

"We Believe in Miracles"
The Story of Father Denis J. Araujo

Just as each of us has one body with many members, and these members do not all have the same function, so in Christ we who are many form one body, and each member belongs to all the others. We have different gifts, according to the grace given us. If a man's gift is prophesying, let him use it in proportion to his faith. If it is serving, let him serve;... if it is showing mercy, let him do it cheerfully.

Romans 12:4-8

Charismatic gifts are those gifts that are found in the members of the body of Christ for the purpose of building up that body. The following story illustrates how the gifts of many people came together to touch the life of a shepherd. As people listened to the Spirit calling, they went to minister in obedience. We can see that the results far exceed anything we can ask or imagine.

Father Denis Araujo moved from India to California in 1956, and became involved in the charismatic renewal in the early 1970s. He was soon a popular, sought-after priest among various charismatic groups.

In June, 1988, when he was seventy years old and serving as pastor at Our Lady of Mercy Church in Richmond, California, he was admitted to Kaiser Hospital in San Francisco for quadruple bypass surgery. He went in confidently, expecting to be home in about a week. While he was in the recovery room, however, he suffered five or six strokes and entered a coma. The doctors painted a grim picture of his future. Even if he came out of the coma, according to the doctors, his brain would be so seriously damaged that he would probably be a vegetable. Family members were advised to discuss the removal of the mechanical life support system.

God had something else in mind, however. During that period he was mobilizing his coworkers for a community miracle. Some of those participants tell their part of the story:

Pat Mullins, The Ephesians 1:4 Prayer Community, Dublin, California. Father Denis was about a week into the coma when Rose Marie Mullins and I went to see him. We were in San Francisco on business, and knew there was a restriction on visitors, but felt that the Lord was directing us to make a visit. We found his room, went in without hindrance, and prayed in tongues over his still form. The Lord gave me a prophecy that he would... use this for his glory; Father Denis would be re-established to full capacity; and he would resume his pastorate. I delivered the prophecy to Father Denis and then we left, our assignment completed. He lay as if dead, with no response.

Juanita Enea, St. Agnes Prayer Group, Concord, California. Father Denis' brother called and told me Father had never regained consciousness, and asked me to go to the hospital and pray. Dr. Zenaida Mendoza and her husband Andy, members of our prayer group, went with me on the first day. We found Father Denis lifeless and on mechanical life support. Sitting in on a family conference with the doctor, we heard a very negative prognosis. At one point I asked, "Doctor, do you believe in miracles?" He responded, "In this case it would take nothing short of a miracle." I said, "We believe in miracles; we want nothing short of a miracle; we want him back to continue his work among us."

Members of our prayer group went daily to the hospital. Gathered around his bed we would pray (and praise) in English and in tongues; we would anoint him (and massage his stiff arms and legs) with oil; we would sing charismatic songs, read Scripture, and pray the rosary. We would talk to his still form, and tell him that he would soon be reading Scripture to us in the Masses he would be celebrating. And we would read out loud his fan mail, which came from India, Canada, the Philippines, Brazil, and many other places around the world.

Things began to happen. One day Dr. Mendoza cleaned Father's mouth with holy water; the next day he began moving his mouth. This encouraged us so much that Isabel, Father's sister-in-law, anointed his eyes with blessed oil from holy places and asked the Lord to open them. The next day his eyes were opened. Vickie and Ernie Ameral from St. Agnes Prayer Group put a green scapular of Mary around his neck. The next day, as we prayed the rosary with Father, we could see him moving his fingers on the rosary we placed in his hand. At that point we knew he was alive and responding to our love and prayers.

On the twelfth day he came out of the coma. One day they removed the life-support, not because he died, but because he no longer needed it. The Lord brought him back.

We shared many special moments with his family as they observed the miracle in process. Even some of the nurses who had observed our actions over the weeks expressed how their faith had been restored or deepened.

Karl and Stephanie Goeppert, St. Agnes Prayer Group. In the visits to the intensive care unit to pray for Father Denis we never once saw defeat in his eyes. One day when I [Stephanie] was standing at the foot of his bed with the team,

Father Denis looked at me with so much love and faith that I gasped and put my hand to my chest. He couldn't speak, but what he communicated was more powerful than words. Even while recuperating in the convalescent hospital, Father Denis took the time to reach out to others with faith and love.

Margaret Richards, Oakland, California. I offered daily Masses for Father Denis, my friend of over thirty years. In addition, I gave him my brown scapular, prayed the rosary for him, and anointed him regularly with holy water from Fatima and Lourdes. His recovery was truly a miracle.

Guy H. Harris, St. Agnes Prayer Group. The physicians stated that if Father Denis survived he would probably be a vegetable. I noted to our friends during a home Mass with Father Denis following his recovery that, "He doesn't look like a turnip to me!" Father Denis' motto has always been, "We are here to serve you." When I think of the times he has gone out of his way to help me, I appreciate all over again his precious servant heart.

Raymond 'Buzz' Tunkel, St. Joseph's Parish, Modesto, California. I first visited Father Denis just after he came out of his coma. He was barely coherent, and curled up like a child. I continued to visit him regularly after he was moved to Richmond, then Vallejo, then the Mercy Care Center, and finally his brother's home. It was a time of extraordinary intimacy, learning to be a servant. There were times when I fed him, shaved him, washed his face, and clipped his toenails. I'm a construction person and have never known that kind of wonderful intimacy with another person. There were times it was inconvenient to stop at his place, but I felt compelled. I had to be there.

I brought Holy Communion regularly, and read verses from the word of God. The Holy Spirit would impress on me, "Read him this psalm, this verse." Sometimes when I arrived he would say, "Buzz, do you have a Scripture for me?" Once I read Romans 8 and he said, "Oh, that is so beautiful...." Another time he said, "Buzz, I want that depth of intimacy with the Lord that you have." We held hands and prayed for him to experience a deeper intimacy with Jesus. I was overwhelmed.

It was a time of absolute, complete surrender, of responding to the Holy Spirit, doing what he told me to do. I did it with no thought of myself; it flowed. Christ flowed through me. I was an instrument of his love for that man. I loved him.

William Arouge, Father Denis' brother. Things were in a terrible state for a couple of months. We thought he was gone. When the doctors spoke of removing my brother from the life-support I said, "No." Even if he was crippled for life, we wanted him back. He was so precious to us. Every day my oldest brother's son, John Arouge, would take off work and drive us to the hospital. We had many sleepless nights praying for Denis. I was amazed at how many people were praying for him. Dozens of calls came in daily from various prayer groups and friends. We brought him home against the advice of the people at the Mercy Center, and saw big changes immediately. He lived with me for six months. I would take him out visiting and walking; my wife would fix him good food.

We recently took him home to India for a visit. He stayed for three months and had a wonderful time. He is presently the second senior priest at St. Isidore's Parish in Danville, California.

Dario Rabak, Bread of Life Prayer Group, Richmond, California. One night during his rehabilitation at Mercy Care Center, our whole prayer group and music ministry ministered to a group of the patients. We sang and gave testimonies and prayed over many of the patients. Father Denis' amazing recovery has had a powerful effect on the whole community. Everyone saw it as a miracle. The doctors said he would never function again. Today his English is better than it was before. He celebrated Mass at his home parish one year after he went into the coma.

Bishop John Cummins, Diocese of Oakland, California. I visited Father Denis twice when he was at Kaiser Hospital in San Francisco. He was in a deep coma the first time. On the second visit, I mentioned his name and he opened his eyes. I said, "Denis, it's the bishop." He formed the word "bishop" with his lips. A few weeks later when I visited him in Vallejo I could not believe the remarkable improvement. Father Denis placed his whole improvement in the prayers of the people who had been faithful with their petitions, and was also sure that the Blessed Mother had a very strong role.

Yolanda Sanders, St. John the Baptist Parish, El Cerrito, California. Father Denis was instrumental in bringing me to the point of conversion to Catholicism, and baptized me into the faith as an adult in 1980. His kindness and compassion during various crises revealed to me the love of God. When I visited him I felt an urgency to reassure him that he was loved and cared for. That care was expressed in various ways. First, I began to massage his legs and feet daily. (He referred to it later as "anointing him with oil.") I felt an inner drive to be there daily. In the physical therapy period I felt an urgency to convince him that he could recover fully. It was a remarkable period, watching him essentially start over. He forgot what peas were, and had to relearn the names of vegetables. He had to relearn his colors. He had to start over in so many ways, and being a part of this learning process for him was a tremendous thing.

This experience has made me very humble. I work as a claims representative for the Social Security Administration and am in daily contact with disabled people. I remember thinking one day, "Suppose I was faced with this situation. Who would take care of me?"

All The Unnamed Intercessors. The miracle came through the prayers of the community; all who loved him and knew him; and those who didn't know him personally, but loved him as a true servant of Jesus and took it on faith that they needed to pray.

Father Denis. Today I am involved in normal parish activities such as celebrating Mass, hearing confessions, and other sacramental functions. In addition, I say home Masses and participate in the prayer group at St. Isidore's as well as the St. Agnes group which meets at Juanita Enea's home.

During the period when I was nearly given up for dead, the Blessed Mother visited me on several occasions. I felt her loving presence, reassurance, and strength. In that same period, Bishop Cummins also visited. Someone told me that he called my name three times and that I seemed to respond, like Lazarus being called back from the dead. This information encouraged the prayer warriors to pray harder.

Looking back over the time of my recovery, I want to say that I had a tremendous trust in Jesus and the Blessed Mother. In some ways I was like a little baby with the Blessed Mother. Perhaps this came from my childhood experience when my mother taught me to kneel, fold my hands, and say the rosary and the Memorare in my native tongue. I would encourage you to memorize this powerful prayer of St. Bernard: "Remember, O most gracious Virgin Mary, that never was it known that anyone who fled to your protection, implored your assistance, or sought your intercession was left unaided. O Virgin of Virgins, my mother, to you I come; before you I kneel, sinful and sorrowful. O Mother of the Word Incarnate, despise not my petitions but in your clemency, hear and answer me. Amen." And this is now my own prayer:

FATHER DENIS' PRAYER

Lord, thank you for sending your people to me in my deepest need. Bless them for their faithfulness, their love, and their courage.

I pray now for those needing a miracle, that they may be filled with the power of the Holy Spirit and believe in the Lord's desire to heal. I say to them now, "Don't give up. Hold onto Jesus. You are safe in him. Trust him to carry you through."

I pray now for those the Lord is calling to reach out to others in need. Lord, tell them how necessary they are. Let them know that they can really make a difference. Oh, Holy Spirit, raise up your people in every city, every state, and every country. Let the world know that Jesus is alive!

SEVENTEEN

M-I-R-A-C-L-E
A Closing Prayer

Living men, you young people and you consecrated souls, you brothers in the priesthood, are you listening to us? This is what the Church needs. She needs the Holy Spirit. The Holy Spirit in us, in each of us, and in all of us together, in us who are the Church.... So let all of you ever say to Him, "Come!" **Pope Paul VI**[1]

M—is for Marvelous. "... great and marvelous are your deeds, Lord God Almighty. Just and true are your ways, King of the ages" (Revelations 15:3). Holy Spirit, thank you for your marvelous touch on Hilario's eyes, on Karen's brain, on Sister Veronica's hernia. Thank you for being the marvelous power in the battery that brought the young girls safely home. Thank you for being Timmy's healing and Noah's life, for holding Phyllis in your heart, for bringing Andy out of drugs and into service, for Charlie's salvation, for giving Cindy the voice to say AABAEE, for sending Evelyn to young Ben, for Patty's little blue flowers. Great and marvelous are your deeds, O King of the ages. Marvelous are your works in the lives of Father Denis, Shirley, and Maria Josephine. You are Mary Ann's wholeness, Shelah's medicine, and Elizabeth's protection on the mountain. Great and marvelous are your deeds, Lord God Almighty. "Since my youth, O God, you have taught me, and to this day I declare your marvelous deeds" (Psalm 71:17).

I—is for Intimacy. "... I am in my Father, and you are in me, and I am in you" (John 14:20). Heavenly Father, thank you for our relationship. The greatest miracle, the greatest gift of all, is knowing you. Through knowing you I enter a new way of life, a life of openness, love, and service, in which miracles are expected and experienced. It all begins with intimacy with you. You are never distant but up close, alongside and inside. In that intimacy I hear and respond to your call to come, listen, learn; to sit, stand, go; to tell, touch, heal; to be your coworker in miracles.

R—is for Resurrection. "'I am the resurrection and the life. He who believes in me will live, even though he dies...' " (John 11:25). Heavenly Father, thank you for allowing your power to flow through us, bringing miracles of healing to sick bodies, minds, and spirits. Thank you for your resurrection power flowing through us to restore families, and deliver people from addictions. Thank you for your power flowing through us to remedy medically hopeless conditions. Thank you for the power to heal cancer, heart disease, emotional wounds, schizophrenia, and all manner of sicknesses and diseases. "Praise be to the God and Father of our Lord Jesus Christ! In his great mercy he has given us new birth into a living hope through the resurrection of Jesus Christ from the dead..." (1 Peter 1:3).

A—is for Ask. " '... ask and it will be given to you; seek and you will find; knock and the door will be opened to you. For everyone who asks receives; he who seeks finds; and to him who knocks, the door will be opened" (Luke 11:9-10). Lord, we have seen how impoverished we are without your power, and we know how rich life can be when your miracles flow freely through the church. We join our prayers with those of Pope John XXIII and ask: "O divine Spirit... renew in our days Your miracles as of a Second Pentecost...."

C—is for Covenant. "'Is not my house right with God? Has he not made with me an everlasting covenant, arranged and secured in every part? Will he not bring to fruition my salvation and grant me my every desire?'" (2 Samuel 23:5). Heavenly Father, you have made an intense personal commitment to me; and I have made an intense personal commitment to you, to the best of my ability. Please bring me to maturity in that covenant. In Jesus' name.

L—is for Love. "And so we know and rely on the love God has for us. God is love. Whoever lives in love lives in God, and God in him" (1 John 4:16). Heavenly Father, knowing that you are love gives me a feeling of safety. I can trust you with my life; I can trust you with those in my care; I can trust you with those in my sphere of influence. Knowing that you are love, I can let go of the barriers of negativity, unlove, unforgiveness, hardness, cynicism, and worldliness. Knowing that you are love, I can bring your love to a hurting world; I can bring your love to those who have hurt me; I can bring your love to my family; I can accept your love for myself. "...and I pray that you, being rooted and established in love, may have power, together with all the saints, to grasp how wide and long and high and deep is the love of Christ, and to know this love that surpasses knowledge—that you may be filled to the measure of all the fullness of God" (Ephesians 3:17-19).

E—is for Eternal Effects. "He has... set eternity in the hearts of men...." (Ecclesiastes 3:11). Heavenly Father, when you touched Paul on the road to Damascus (Acts 9), he became one of the greatest evangelists in history. When you touched

Peter, James, and John, they left everything and followed you. When you touched the known and unknown saints of history, their lives were forever changed. When you touched the people who shared their stories in this book, their lives were lifted up into a new sphere. They caught a glimpse of eternity, and life was never quite the same again.

Knowing this, my faith should be perfect. Yet I hang my head and confess that there is still something in me that responds like doubting Thomas, who said, "... unless I see the nail marks in his hands and put my finger where the nails were, and put my hand into his side, I will not believe it," (John 20:25). As I confess this weakness, I sense your forgiving whisper, "... put your finger here; see my hands. Reach out your hand and put it into my side. Stop doubting and believe," (v. 27). With Thomas, I now fall to my knees and say, "... my Lord and my God!" (v. 28).

Notes

ONE
Longing for Miracles

1. John XXIII, *Journal of a Soul* (New York: McGraw Hill, 1965) 391.
2. Rene Laurentin, *Miracles in El Paso?* (Ann Arbor: Servant Publications, 1982) 86.
3. "Dogmatic Constitution on the Church," *The Documents of Vatican II*, edited by Walter M. Abbott, S.J. (New York: American Press, 1966) No. 12.
4. Robert DeGrandis, S.S.J., *Praying for Miracles: A Workbook Approach* (Lowell: Heart of Mary Books, 1990).

TWO
What Is a Miracle?

1. "Dogmatic Constitution on the Church," *The Documents of Vatican II*, edited by Walter M. Abbott, S.J. (New York: American Press, 1966) No. 12.
2. Henricus Denzinger and Adolfus Schonmetzre, S.I., editors, *Enchiridion Symbolorum: Definitionum et Declarationum de Rebus Fidei et Morum* (Barcelona: Herder, 1976) paragraph 3009.
3. Ibid., paragraph 3034.
4. "Dogmatic Constitution on the Church," *The Documents of Vatican II*, edited by Walter M. Abbott, S.J. (New York: American Press, 1966) No. 5.

5. Louis Monden, *Signs and Wonders* (New York: Descler Company, 1966)94.

6. Patricia Treece, *Nothing Short of a Miracle: The Healing Power of the Saints* (New York: Doubleday Image Books, 1988) xxiv-xxv.

7. Joan Carroll Cruz, *The Incorruptibles* (Rockford: Tan Books and Publishers, Inc., 1977) 103, 139, 149, 172, 250, 256.

8. Treece, xxx.

9. Cruz, 294, 296, 297.

10. *Webster's Seventh New Collegiate Dictionary* (Springfield: G & C Merriam Co., 1963) 540.

11. Albert J. Nevins, compiler and editor, *Maryknoll Catholic Dictionary*, first American edition (New York: Grosset and Dunlap, 1965) s.v. "miracle," 374.

12. Merrill F. Unger, editor *Unger's Bible Dictionary*, Third Edition (Chicago: Moody press, 1966) 747.

13. W.E. Vine, *Vine's Expository Dictionary of Old and New Testament Words* (Old Tappan: Fleming H. Revell Co., 1981) 75.

14. Msgr. Vincent M. Walsh, *Lead my People* (Philadelphia: Key of David Publications, 1980) 50.

THREE
Characteristics of Miracles

1. Paul VI, Address to General Audience, November 29, 1972 (translated from "L'Osservatore Romano," English language edition) December 7, 1972, 1.

2. Robert DeGrandis, S.S.J., *Intergenerational Healing* (Lowell: Heart of Mary Books, 1989) 18, 45, 47.

3. Robert DeGrandis, S.S.J., *Coming to Life* (Lowell:Hom Books) 24.

FOUR
Miracle Covenants

1. Paul VI, "The Holy Spirit and the Life of the Church," General Audience, October 12, 1966 (translated from *The Pope Speaks* [Washington, D.C., 1962] 12) 79-81.

2. "Dogmatic Constitution on Divine Revelation," *The Documents of Vatican II*, edited by Walter M. Abbott, S.J. (New York: American Press, 1966) No. 14.

FIVE
Miracles through the Centuries

1. Pope Paul IV, Address to General Audience, November 29, 1972 (translated from "L'Osservatore Romano," English language edition) December 7, 1972, 1.
2. The following quotes are taken from the leaflet, *Signs and Wonders: God Among Us*, by Daniel F. Stramara, O.S.B. (Pecos: Dove Publications) December, 1987.
3. Father Emilien Tardif, *Jesus is Alive* (South Bend: Greenlawn Press, 1990).
4. Rene Laurentin, *Miracles in El Paso?* (Ann Arbor: Servant Publications, 1982).

SIX
Yielding—The Secret of Miracle Power

1. Pope Paul VI, "The Holy Spirit and the Life of the Church," Gerenal Audience, October 12,1966 (Tr. from *The Pope Speaks* [Washington, D.C.] : 12, 1967) 79.
2. Briege McKenna, O.S.C., *Miracles Do Happen* (Ann Arbor: Servant Publications, 1987) 39-40.

SEVEN
Responding—Action Step to Miracles

1. "Decree on the Apostolate of the Laity," *The Documents of Vatican II*, edited by Walter M. Abbot, S.J. (New York: American Press, 1966) No. 3.

EIGHT
Questions and Answers

1. "Dogmatic Constitution on the Church," *The Documents of Vatican II*, edited by Walter M. Abbot, S.J. (New York: American Press, 1966) No. 34.
2. "Decree on the Apostolate of the Laity," *The Documents of Vatican II*, No. 3.
3. Rene Laurentin, *Miracles in El Paso?* (Ann Arbor: Servant Publications, 1982) 93-94.
4. Laurentin, 1.
5. Laurentin, 85.

NINE
Do You Believe?

1. Paul VI, "The Holy Spirit and the Life of the Church," General Audience, October 12, 1966 (Tr. from *The Pope Speaks* [Washington, D.C.] : 12) 80.
2. Agnes Sanford, *The Healing Light* (Plainfield: Logos International, 1972).
3. Francis MacNutt, *Healing* (Notre Dame: Ave Maria Press, 1974).
4. Laurentin, *Miracles in El Paso?* (Ann Arbor: Servant Publications, 1982) 110-111.

ELEVEN
His Word Is Life

1. Testimony of John H. Hampsch, C.M.F., *Riding High* (Claretian Tape Ministry, P.O. Box 19100, Los Angeles, CA 90019-0100).

TWELVE
"I'm Not Afraid of the Morning Anymore"

1. The 'forgiveness prayer' is one that covers most relationships. I have found this prayer to be the best method of bringing to mind people one needs to forgive. It is printed in eight languages and has received acclaim from many countries as a powerful instrument of bringing people to deep forgiveness of others as well as themselves. Deep forgiveness opens people to healing. The prayer is printed in many of my books as a standard way of bringing people into healing. See page 105 for the text of this prayer.

SEVENTEEN
M-I-R-A-C-L-E

1. Pope Paul IV, "The Breath of the Holy Spirit" in *The Teachings of Pope Paul IV, 1972* (Washington, D.C. : U.S. Catholic Conference, 1973) 175,177.

The Miracles of Jesus, Peter, and Paul

THE MIRACLES OF JESUS

The afflicted child—Matthew 17:14, Mark 9:17, Luke 9:37

The blind Bartimaeus—Mark 10:46

The blind man of Bethsaida—Mark 8:23

The Canaanite woman's daughter—Matthew 15:22, Mark 7:25

Catching fish—Luke 5:6, John 21:6

The centurion's servant—Matthew 8:5, Luke 7:2

Changing the water into wine—John 2:9

Cleansing the leper—Matthew 8:2, Mark 1:41, Luke 5:12

Cursing the fig tree—Matthew 21:19

The deaf and dumb man—Mark 7:32

Feeding the five thousand—Matthew 14:15, Mark 6:41, Luke 9:12, John 6:5

Feeding the four thousand—Matthew 15:32, Mark 8:8

Freeing the blind and mute demoniac—Mathew 12:22

Freeing the demoniac in the synagogue—Mark 1:25, Luke 4:35

Freeing the demoniac who was mute—Matthew 9:32

Freeing the demoniacs of Gadara—Matthew 8:28, Mark 5:1, Luke 8:26

Freeing the mute demoniac—Luke 11:14
The high priest's servant—Luke 22:50
His resurrection—Luke 24:6
The invalid—John 5:5
The man born blind—John 9:1
The man with dropsy—Luke 14:2
The man with the shriveled hand—Matthew 12:10, Mark 3:1, Luke 6:6
The nobleman's son—John 4:46
The paralytic—Matthew 9:2, Mark 2:3, Luke 5:18
Peter's mother-in-law—Matthew 8:14, Mark 1:30, Luke 4:38
Raising of Jairus' daughter—Matthew 9:18, Mark 5:35, Luke 8:41
Raising of Lazarus—John 11
Raising the widow's son—Luke 7:11
Stilling the storm—Matthew 8:23, Mark 4:35, Luke 8:22
Temple tax—Matthew 17:24
The ten lepers—Luke 17:12
The two blind men—Matthew 9:27, Matthew 20:30
Walking on the water—Matthew 14:25, Mark 6:47, John 6:19
The woman with the hemorrhage—Matthew 9:20, Mark 5:25, Luke 8:43
The woman with the spirit of infirmity—Luke 13:10

MIRACLES OF PETER

Lame man cured—Acts 3:7
Ananias and Sapphira—Acts 5:5, 10
Sick healed—Acts 5:15
Aeneas—Acts 9:34
Tabitha—Acts 9:40

MIRACLES OF PAUL

Elymas blinded—Acts 13:11
General account of miracles—Acts 14:3
Lame man cured—Acts 14:8
Girl with spirit of divination—Acts 16:16
General account of miracles—Acts 19:11
Eutychus restored to life—Acts 20:9
Viper's bite—Acts 28:3
Father of Publius healed—Acts 28:7